I Will
Find You

I Will
Find You

JOANNA
CONNORS

FOURTH ESTATE • *London*

Fourth Estate
a division of HarperCollins*Publishers*
1 London Bridge Street
London SE1 9GF
www.4thestate.co.uk

First published in Great Britain in 2016 by Fourth Estate

First published in the United States in 2016 by
Atlantic Monthly Press, an imprint of Grove Atlantic

A catalogue record for this book is
available from the British Library

ISBN (HB) 978-0-00-818182-6
ISBN (TPB) 978-0-00-752185-2

Epigraph quote by James Baldwin from "As Much Truth As One Can Bear," *The New York Times*
(January 14, 1962). Quote on p. 76 from Ovid's *Metamorphoses*, translated by Rolfe Humphries
(Indiana University Press, 1955), 146–48. Quote on p. 115 by James Baldwin from "Lorraine
Hansberry at the Summit," *Freedomways* 19:4 (1979) 269–72.

Every effort has been made to trace copyright holders and to obtain their permission for the
use of copyright material. The publisher apologizes for any errors or omissions and would
be grateful if notified of any corrections that should be incorporated in future reprints
or editions of this book.

Printed and bound in Great Britain by
Clays Ltd, St Ives plc

MIX
Paper from
responsible sources
FSC
www.fsc.org   **FSC® C007454**

FSC™ is a non-profit international organisation established to promote
the responsible management of the world's forests. Products carrying the
FSC label are independently certified to assure consumers that they come
from forests that are managed to meet the social, economic and
ecological needs of present and future generations,
and other controlled sources.

Find out more about HarperCollins and the environment at
www.harpercollins.co.uk/green

For Dan and Zoe, beloved
And for Chris, who went through it with me

Author's Note

It's no surprise that the term "Rashomon effect" comes from a movie about a rape and murder. Akira Kurosawa's masterpiece (based on the work of Ryūnosuke Akutagawa) tells the story of a violent encounter in the woods through the testimony of four characters. Each one recounts a different version of what happened—including the murdered samurai, who testifies through a medium.

"Rashomon effect" has become shorthand for the way perspective can alter memory. Neuroscientific research suggests that memory is not solid. It is capricious and highly susceptible to outside influence, and changes with each retrieval from the brain.

The addition of trauma makes memory the ultimate unreliable narrator of our own past.

I fact-checked my memories in this book with as much evidence as possible, including stacks of documents, dozens of recorded interviews, and my own journals.

But I also relied on my memories. Others who experienced this trauma may, like the woodcutter or the wife in *Rashomon*, have other perspectives and other stories to tell. To honor their privacy, I have changed the names of some of the people in this book, and changed characteristics that might identify them.

"Not everything that is faced can be changed,
but nothing can be changed until it is faced."
—James Baldwin

I Will
Find You

CHAPTER ONE

"Be it remembered"

I was thirty years old when I left my body for the first time.

When it happened, I had not taken any drugs, not for a couple of years. I was sober, it was the middle of the day, I was working, and I did not believe out-of-body reports any more than I believed a man could bend a spoon with his mind.

I worked for a newspaper, where facts mattered and skepticism was essential, and I tried to develop the cynicism I saw in older reporters while praying no one would figure out I was a fraud who had no business being in a newsroom.

I had just moved to Cleveland from Minneapolis to start work at *The Plain Dealer*, the city's daily paper, and, as it proclaimed in the front-page banner, "Ohio's Largest Newspaper." It was my second job in what amounted to the family trade. My grandfather had worked at *The Knickerbocker News* in Albany, New York, my father was a reporter and editor at the *Miami Herald* when I was a girl, and I had worked at the *Minneapolis Star* (now the *Star Tribune*) before going to Cleveland.

I had resisted following in my father's wake until I was nineteen. I didn't want his career. By then, he was a magazine editor, and I was determined to separate myself from everything about my parents and their suburban lives. On visits home, I used the term "bourgeois" a lot. I was very young.

The only reason I walked into my college newspaper to ask for a job was because my sister Nancy worked there and told me they paid ten cents a column inch. I found my career and met my husband in that little basement newsroom, where I discovered that newspaper work takes you places you'd never get to go otherwise, and introduces you to people you would never come near without a press pass. Even better, newspaper people know how to have fun. I learned that early in life, when I was seven years old and my parents had a *Miami Herald* party in our backyard. I stayed up late with my sister, peeking through the window, watching them drink and laugh and flirt and, when it got very late, jump into the pool naked. My parents didn't get naked, which would be too disturbing to recall, but the party did end dramatically, with my mother stepping on a broken glass and having to go to the hospital for stitches in her foot. I remember one of the men saying, "I'll just pour some gin on it, Susie," and my mother shouting, "No!" and everybody laughing. This frightened and thrilled me in equal measure.

Going to work in a newsroom used to be like going to a cocktail party every day, with all your clothes on and without the booze or the blood. Usually. Every newspaper has its feuds, gossip, and vanity; most have a legend or two of a newsroom brawl. At *The Plain Dealer*, people swore that a reporter once threw a typewriter—a heavy electric one—at an editor and then left the building, never to return. Everyone remembered the fight; no one remembered the reason for it.

Cynicism is both a badge of honor and a professional liability. Newspaper people don't start out that way; almost everyone I know started out as an idealist wanting to bring justice to an unjust world. Cynicism seeps in over time, a slow acidic leak that erodes the idealism, the natural result of being told lies all day long, of calls not returned and records withheld, of corners cut to get a story in on time.

So I did not believe that out-of-body experiences were real. And yet: At 4:30 p.m. on a hot July afternoon, on a college campus in Cleveland, Ohio, I slipped away from my body and rose, up and up, until I was hovering somewhere in the air.

I looked down at the stage of a small theater, where I was on my knees in front of a man who held a long, rusty blade to my neck and was ordering me to suck on his penis.

"Suck on it," he said, pushing on my head.

From my perch above this scene, I watched with a calm I'd never felt before.

It had come in an instant, this leaving my body. It happened as soon as I saw my own blood on my hand. The blood stunned me. I had not felt a cut, just the cool metal at my throat, as the man dragged me across the stage, but I didn't know he had used it until a few minutes later, when I put my hand to my neck. It felt sticky.

I looked at my hand, and saw a smear of red.

Dread struck at once, slithering through my chest and into my stomach. I felt its venom spread outward, through my limbs, and then up into my throat. The poison worked in quick stages: shock, then panic, then paralysis.

By the time my brain began to work again, I was looking at myself from high above, up in the theater's fly space among the ropes and lights. From that vantage point, I watched the man rape me.

I observed with an odd detachment. It was as though what was happening on that stage was happening to someone else. I was viewing a Hollywood thriller, and we had come to the inevitable rape scene. They were actors; I was the audience.

The woman on the stage looked up at the man. She moved in slow motion.

"Suck on it," he said again. "I got to get off."

I wondered when he would kill the woman. Not whether he would do it, but when. I knew it would happen, the way you know certain secondary characters will be killed in a movie. From my position above, I accepted it as a necessary plot element.

I was not sad, or scared, hovering up there. If anything, I was curious. How would he do it? What would I feel?

I understood that the girl on her knees was alone, but soon she would not be. She would join all the other girls who had been raped and then killed. I wondered if this was how they felt when it happened to them. Detached. Alone. Floating out of time.

All those dead, lovely girls. I still think of them, all the time.

We printed their high-school graduation pictures in our newspaper, their faces turned and tilted by the photographer so that they seemed to be gazing toward a future they had just started to imagine, their long hair so shiny you could practically smell the Herbal Essences shampoo when you looked at them.

Our editors sent reporters and photographers to the woods and roadside ditches where sheriff's deputies were digging, where the girls had lain, ever patient, waiting to be found. The reporters interviewed their keening mothers while the silent fathers, stunned by loss and fury, tried to comfort them. The reporters took their graduation pictures back to the newsroom, and when the time came they covered the trials of the men who killed them. If the time came.

And then, a week or a month later, we forgot them. We went on to the next one. There was always a next one.

I pictured all the girls together, somewhere. Maybe they were watching this happen, just as I was, and waiting for me.

★

I guess you could call this the story of a quest. When it all started, though, I didn't think of it as one. The great quest stories all revolved around men—men going off into unknown lands on brave adventures. Kings and gods sent them off on their journeys, sometimes giving them magic swords. Poets sang of them, telling stories of heroes who sailed ships on wine-dark seas, rode over mountains on the backs of elephants, searched for holy treasure, rescued beautiful women.

I was a middle-aged, middle-class working mother, living in the suburbs of Cleveland, Ohio, a woman who once thought of herself as fearless but now was afraid of just about everything.

I did not undertake journeys. When I had a choice, I rarely left my house.

This was not how I always was. There was a time when I hitchhiked everywhere, when everyone I knew did, too, feeling a reckless thrill whenever a car pulled over and the passenger door opened and we ran to it, not knowing who would be sitting in the driver's seat. I walked alone in the dark, everywhere, breaking the rule girls learn early in life from the Grimm Brothers: Never venture into the dark forest alone. At sixteen, I decided that rule did not apply to me. If a man could do it, then I should be able to do it, too.

What happened to that headstrong girl? Whenever I thought about her, I felt a wave of melancholy. I missed her.

Now I was afraid of sitting in a movie theater. Since I was by that time the film critic for my paper, this made my job complicated. When I went to a screening alone, which happened fairly often in a one-newspaper town, I sat with all my muscles clenched, struggling to focus on the movie. I finally asked the theater managers to lock the doors on me, which they did, though it must have broken fire department regulations. With this and countless other silly but imperative solutions, I organized my life to avoid risk.

I also became practiced at avoiding everything to do with the rape. After it was all over, after I had told the police and the doctors and the prosecutor and judge and jury, after they'd sent the rapist to prison for a long time, I stopped talking about it. I took what had happened and buried it inside myself, as deep as I could. I didn't tell my friends. I didn't tell my two children when they were old enough to hear it. I didn't talk about it anymore with my husband or sisters or mother. I told them, and myself, that I was fine. Fine! Just fine.

But here's the thing I discovered: I might have buried this story, but it was not dead. I had buried it alive, and it grew in that deep place I put it, like a vine from some mutant seed, all twisted and ugly and tenacious as kudzu. As it grew, it strangled a lot of other stuff in me that should have been growing. It killed my courage and joy. It killed my trust in the world.

Worse, the vine reached out to entangle my children. When I was raped, I was married but I did not have children yet. My son was born a year and a half after the rape, my daughter a couple of years after that. But even though they were not alive when it happened, research shows that they inherited my rape and the terror that came with it. They lived in its twisted grip with me.

I was always waiting for something terrible to happen to them. I imagined those terrible things in documentary detail. Car accidents. Kidnappers. Pedophiles. Murderers. They filled my brain like the inventory in a torture chamber. When Eric Clapton's "Tears in Heaven" came out and I read the backstory—he wrote it for his four-year-old son, who fell to his death from an apartment window—the song became the inner sound track to my days. I imagined these things and rehearsed my grief, which always ended the same way: I would not be able to go on.

I would not write a beautiful song about them. I would not make art or sense out of their death. I would jump out of the window right after them.

I knew all parents worry about safety. The minute they are born, our children make us all hostages to fortune. But these parents considered the dangers in the world and figured out ways to avoid them. They baby-proofed their kitchens and medicine cabinets; they kept their eye on their children when they played outside and made sure they wore helmets when they learned to ride a bicycle.

I was not one of those reasonable parents. I baby-proofed our entire lives, putting locks on everything, including the children themselves.

I hovered and fretted over them nonstop, zooming to red alert if I heard a random shriek when they played in the backyard. When they went for a sleepover at a friend's house, I stayed awake all night, waiting for the emergency call from the hospital.

When I returned to work six months after my son was born, we hired a babysitter, an affectionate middle-aged woman with a musical voice and a lap like a pillow. She made our baby son giggle when she arrived each morning.

I had checked her references, but, based on nothing, I felt uneasy about her. At work, I worried about what she might do to my son. This was before nanny cams, but if they had existed I would have mounted one in every corner of the house.

I asked my husband, who was then a police reporter at the paper, to do a criminal-records check on her. In most states it's easy to access these public records now, online, but in 1985 it involved an in-person visit to the Clerk of Courts.

When he turned up nothing, I was not reassured. One night I followed her home and parked on the street, watching her apartment windows like a cop on a stakeout. Then I went to see her boss at the nearby mall, where she worked every Saturday and Sunday night, cleaning after the stores closed. He refused to tell me anything about her, even when I started crying. I left, hating him, and the next day I let her go. I couldn't get over my fear that she would hurt my son.

I started working at home, where I could keep an eye on the new babysitter we hired. A friend had recommended her. I began to nurture suspicions about her, too.

My dark thoughts spread. For a time, I even imagined my husband might be abusing our son. I had no evidence of this, none at all. My husband loved our son more than he loved me, but it didn't matter that I had no reason to suspect him. I hated leaving him alone with my baby. Once I left to do errands and returned ten minutes later, much sooner than I'd said I would, thinking I would catch him in the act. They were outside, sitting on the grass, examining an earthworm.

I was aware that this was not normal. I suspected that I was close to being delusional. Even so, I could not turn it off. I couldn't tell anyone about these fears, either. I knew it would make me look crazy—I was sane enough to see that, at least.

So I turned my life into performance art. I acted normal, or as normal as I could manage, all the while living on my secret island of fear. As time went on, the list of my fears continued to grow. I was afraid of flying. Afraid of driving. Afraid of riding in a car while someone else drove. Afraid of driving over bridges. Afraid of elevators. Afraid of enclosed spaces. Afraid of the dark. Afraid of going into crowds. Afraid of being alone. Afraid, most of all, to let my children out of my sight.

From the outside, my performance worked. I looked and acted like most other mothers. Only I knew that my entire body vibrated with dread, poised to flee when necessary.

I suppose it's lucky I realized I was on a quest only when it was almost over.

It began on another college campus, twenty-one years after my rape. It was 2005, a time when the world seemed to be collapsing. That summer, terrorists had attacked three trains and a bus in London, murdering fifty-two people and injuring seven hundred. A series of terrorist bombs in Bali killed twenty-six people. In the United States, Hurricane Katrina hit in August, leading to the deaths of almost two thousand people in the aftermath of flooding and violence, and destroying much of New Orleans, the Gulf Coast, and Americans' sense of trust in the fairness of our government. I was feeling, along with the rest of the country, a new form of anxiety about the future. It felt like we were all standing on a precipice.

That fall, my son left for his second year of college and my daughter started her last year of high school.

The schools had been prepping the kids since third grade for college admissions, and when October came, it was time for her Big College Tour—a ritual that puts teenagers and their parents in a car together for several days, where they bond over the shared conviction that it really is time for the teenager to go away from home for a while.

We were on Day Two, at college number three or four. Zoë was in that senior-year stage where half the time she was so impatient and annoyed with me that I couldn't wait for her to leave and take her sighs and silences with her, and half the time she was the sweet, funny little girl who used to squiggle down under the covers with me at night, or play Dolphin in the Pool. In those games, I was her trainer, feeding her pretend fish for each somersault she did below the surface, her little body slipping like mercury through the water.

Sweet Zoë was on this trip, keeping me laughing and choosing all the CDs as we drove, a heavy rotation of Modest Mouse's CD, *Good News for People Who Love Bad News*. Appropriate. Zoë's good mood might have had something to do with the three days she was taking off from school. Still, I was surprised that she was walking with me on the campus tours rather than ten yards behind me, the way my son had on his tours. Dan had hung back with the other kids who were concentrating on the sidewalks, pretending they did not know those dorks ahead of them in the unfortunate mom jeans— who, I want to point out, included many of the dads. It didn't help when I knocked over an entire row of bicycles, domino style, at one of the recreation centers.

"Sorry!" I kept saying as I tried to put twenty-five bikes back on their stands. "Sorry!"

When I looked around, Dan had vanished. I didn't blame him.

But Zoë was with me all the way. She was making me miss her before she even packed the first of the sixty-three boxes of stuff she took with her the next year. All of this made me feel unexpectedly buoyant. I had loved everything about college, especially the going-away-from-home part. I even skipped my senior year in high school to get there a year early. The University of Minnesota was where I found myself and my tribe, that day I walked into the subterranean offices of the *Minnesota Daily*, the college paper, and asked for a job. Half the staff was in the darkroom, smoking a joint. The rest of them were sitting around talking about Hunter S. Thompson. Everyone wanted to do his gonzo journalism that year, or imitate Tom Wolfe's new journalism, and since the students controlled the paper, a lot of them did. It made for unusual coverage of the Board of Regents meetings.

The rain started just as Zoë and I pulled into the visitors' lot at Clark University in Worcester, Massachusetts, a college best known for its psychology program, which she had decided was where she wanted her life to go. When Sigmund Freud made his first and only trip to America, in 1909, he went to Clark to deliver his famous lectures. A life-size bronze statue of Freud, deep in thought, sits on a bench on the campus.

Inside the admissions office, a cluster of parents at the windows murmured about whether to do the tour in the rain or skip it. Zoë wanted to see the campus, so when the tour guide called out that it was time to start, we buttoned up our jackets, opened our one umbrella, and fell in with the swarm of parents and seniors.

Our guide, a skinny boy with fogged-up glasses, walked backward and ignored the rain, which had started as a drizzle but now came down steady and cold. We stopped to see the same things we'd seen at the last campus: a dorm and a dorm room, the cafeteria, the gym. By this point, the tour had sustained several dropouts.

"Now we'll head over to the library," the guide said.

At the back of the crowd, Zoë and I held the umbrella between us, the rain dribbling down her right side and my left. We lurched along, like mismatched partners in a three-legged race.

"Listen, I'm prepared to take it on absolute faith that every university does, in fact, have a library," I said. "I don't need to see to believe."

Zoë smiled, but she also sighed. I recognized that sigh as my own when I was seventeen, a sign that the mother-daughter bonding was coming unglued.

I was about to suggest cutting away from the group and going for coffee when the guide stopped on the path. Freud sat nearby, awaiting what had been building up inside me for two decades to emerge. He knew more than I did.

The guide gestured to a glowing light and said, "You've probably noticed these blue lights around campus. They're safety stations. If you're walking alone at night and you think someone is following you, or you might be in danger, you get to one of these blue lights, call, and help will be there within five minutes."

All the parents nodded, reassured.

Those parents were idiots.

"Five minutes?" I whispered to Zoë. "Who are they kidding? Five minutes is too late. Way too late. You could be dead in five minutes."

Zoë, who remembers it now as a stage whisper that everyone heard, looked at me for a long pause, shook her head, and went on with the group, leaving me standing alone beneath the blue light.

I watched her walk away, the hem of her jeans dragging on the wet pavement. I felt the same way I always feel when I look at her: amazed that this girl, so unlike me, is my daughter. Zoë was like the girls I envied at that age, the girls who blazed through the halls of my high school, while I thought only about cutting class and going anywhere else. She was strong, confident, smart, beautiful. She was funny. She was not afraid to speak her mind and ask for what she wanted.

I looked at my daughter and saw a young woman who was ready to go out into the world and make it her own. But now I saw something else, too.

She was prey.

I was sending her to a campus. I could see her standing in a pool of blue light on a dark path, scared, alone, calling for help, watching a man walk toward her while she waited for someone to come save her.

She had five minutes.

The venomous snake returned, slithering through my body. Panic dropped from my chest to my gut so fast I thought I might throw up. My vision blurred and narrowed, dark at the edges. The ordinary campus sounds around me turned into a muffled roar in my ears. I dropped the umbrella and grabbed the post with the blue light with both hands, willing myself to keep standing.

Then I felt myself float up into the air like a balloon escaping from a child's fist. I saw the middle-aged woman below, rain dripping off her hair into her face.

I was back at that other campus, twenty-one years before, suspended high above a stage and looking down at myself.

★

That was our last college tour. I couldn't walk any more blue-lighted pathways that week. As we drove west, back to Cleveland, we didn't talk much.

I clocked the miles asking myself the question: *Should I tell them?* One mile I would think, *Yes, now they are old enough.* The next I would think, *No, no matter how old they are, it's too much for children to think of their mother with a knife at her throat.* A few miles on, I would think, *But I need to warn Zoë. I can't let her go by herself to a college campus without knowing what can happen there.* This was several years before campus rape became a widely discussed and reported issue, and I was not thinking of the dangers she faced by simply going on a date, or to a party at a fraternity house—dangers that, statistically, were far more prevalent than encountering strangers in empty buildings.

And so it went, through Massachusetts and New York, along Lake Erie into Pennsylvania and finally Ohio, Zoë listening to Modest Mouse and singing along.

★

How do you tell your children a story you never want them to hear? How do you explain how it made you the mother you were?

This is why I hovered over you. This is why my internal alarm clanged constantly, why I treated every tumble and scrape as an emergency, and every sleepover party as a potential kidnapping situation. I wanted you to embrace the world and live boldly, but I worry that my actions taught you to fear the world and not trust anyone. I hope this will explain my thousand-yard stare, the one you hated because it meant I was not paying attention. I hope it explains all those times I vanished into myself and you waved your hands in front of my face, saying, "Mom!"

Can you forgive me?

The pendulum swung from yes to no for two weeks. When I finally stopped it on a yes, I should tell them, I decided to do it in the car. A friend once told me that that's the best place to have difficult conversations with your kids. "They're trapped with you," she explained. "So they have to listen. But you aren't facing each other, so it's easier. Less confrontational. Let them pick the music, too."

I wanted to tell them separately, so on the Wednesday before Thanksgiving, I talked Zoë into driving to Cincinnati with me to pick up Dan from school. I would tell her on the way down. I would wait and tell Dan on another car trip.

We left early, driving south under a low, leaden sky. Rain hit the windshield in icy splotches that would turn into sleet, and then snow. All of Ohio seemed to be going the same direction, the holiday traffic forming a funereal procession on the slippery highway. The car felt like a cozy refuge as we drove through the open farmland and fog-shrouded valleys. South of Columbus, we came to the black billboard that looms over the highway going south, announcing "HELL IS REAL" in giant white letters. On the return highway north, two identical black billboards list the Ten Commandments, five on each billboard.

The "HELL" sign lets you know you're close to Cincinnati. It was time.

How did I put it? Not long ago, I asked Zoë what she remembered of that day.

"You said, 'I have something I want to tell you,'" she told me. "You kind of scared me. I thought maybe you were going to say Grammy had died, or you and Dad were getting divorced."

After that she didn't remember, and I didn't, either. I probably said an awkward and pause-filled version of, "I was raped when I was thirty years old, on a college campus, and it scares me that you're going to college." That's what I know I felt: I had to tell her what had happened to me as a kind of magical insurance policy, so it would never happen to her.

We both remember that she started crying, almost instantly. Not the vocal kind of crying, but the kind she inherited from me, silent and stricken, our chins trembling and our eyes filling with tears until they spill over and run down our cheeks.

I told her the story I had told so often in the hours and days after the rape: I was working, I was late for an interview, the building was empty, the guy was there, he cut me on the throat. I didn't talk about what he did to me after that.

I remember clearly one thing she said. "Now I see why you and Dad were so overprotective. Especially Dad."

This was news to me. I thought I was the one driving them crazy with my hovering. I was so wrapped up in my fears, I hadn't even noticed that my husband was tied up in his own knots of worry and fear over our children.

"Really?" I said, looking over at her.

"Sometimes it feels like you guys are stalking me," she said.

★

I told Dan a few months later, when I picked him up for summer break. This time I drove to Cincinnati alone, thinking the whole way about how and why he had come into the world.

It occurred to me that he was a child born out of my fear.

The night I was raped, twenty-one years before, my husband took me home from the hospital to a bare house, a center-hall colonial built in 1927 in Shaker Heights. We had just moved into it, our first house after years of apartments, and we had no furniture for three of the four bedrooms, let alone the two extra bedrooms on the third floor. Our parents joked that we had to do something to fill all those rooms up. Meaning children.

But I wasn't sure I wanted children, and the "not-sure" teetered toward "never." I hated babysitting when I was a teenager. I avoided other people's children at parties, and if someone forced a baby into my arms, it never failed to start wailing. Those twinges of yearning women call baby lust? I never felt them.

Freud wrote that we cannot truly imagine our own death. "Whenever we try to do so we find that we survive ourselves as spectators," he wrote. "At bottom, no one believes in his own death, which amounts to saying: In the unconscious every one of us is convinced of his immortality."

But I was no longer convinced. I had glimpsed my own death in a gloomy theater, in a smear of my own blood, and it changed everything. I lay awake through the nights, aching with the knowledge of what Harold Brodkey called "this wild darkness." While my husband slept next to me, I started thinking about what I wanted from this too-short life. I began to think about having a child. I hate the drugstore perfume of sentimentality, but one thought broke through my barricades: I could push back death by bringing life into my life.

By the anniversary of the rape, I was pregnant. My son was born October 7, 1985, eleven days after his due date, no more ready for this than I was. We named him Daniel and gave him my last name as his middle name. The nurses cleaned him up before they handed him to me, wrapped like a burrito in a blanket, showing only a thick head of black hair and a face all battered and bruised from the suction-cup delivery that came after a thirty-six-hour labor—a story I would repeat probably way too often in the coming years, usually on Dan's birthdays. Lucky boy.

The labor ended only when the doctor gave me the thing all journalists must have: a deadline. Deliver within two hours, she said, or we do a C-section. With the help of copious drugs and the suction device, I delivered. When the nurse presented him to us, my husband said, "He looks like he was mugged on his way here."

When I held my bruised baby, my heart cracked into a mosaic of intense love, opiate-fueled bliss, and hideous, morbid fear. I felt like the mother in "Sleeping Beauty," cradling my child against the curse of a jealous witch.

My husband took my tears to be of happiness, and I let him think it. He sat next to me on the hospital bed, and we passed our burrito baby back and forth as we admired him. He looked back at us. We cooed.

And then he looked right at me and said, "Hi." He really did. We both heard it, and nothing will ever persuade us it was just a burp.

Once home from the hospital, I started crying and could not stop. I wept as I nursed my son, filling him with milk laced with my anxieties as I watched my tears drizzle down my breast. It did not take long for him to begin crying, crying endlessly, cramped with colic and the calamitous fears I fed him. We cried together. I wept alone in bed. I wept in the shower and I wept at the dinner table while my husband, my mother, and my stepfather sat in silence, heads down, the food going cold.

"I'm fine!" I kept telling them. I tried to form a smile. "I don't know why I'm crying!" And I really didn't know why. I had a healthy baby who would be beautiful as soon as his birth bruises faded and he stopped crying. I had a home, a job, a husband who loved me.

My mother, who had arrived in Cleveland before I was even out of the hospital, patted my back as I wept and told me all I needed was a good long sleep.

"Let me get up with him for a few nights and feed him from a bottle," she said. "We can put his cradle in my room."

I heard this kind offer as if it were a threat to kidnap my baby.

I was still weeping when my mother and stepfather left, still weeping when the other grandparents arrived, still weeping when they left, still saying, "I'm fine!"

Two weeks passed this way. My husband went back to work. That first morning, I sat on the couch in the quiet, my baby on my lap. We were alone.

One of the twenty-six baby books I was consulting at the time advised parents to keep up a steady stream of conversation with their baby. I looked at Danny on my lap, and he looked back at me. He had that look of intense, worried concentration babies sometimes get. He was ready to listen, but I didn't have anything to say. What did the book mean by "having a conversation" with an infant?

I propped him up a little higher on my leg and gave it a try. "So here we are," I said. "You and me." We stared at each other in silence. I pressed on. "I want you to know that I will always be here."

Now he looked puzzled. "I am your mother," I explained, "and you will always have me. I will always love you. I will protect you, and I promise I will never, ever let anything bad happen to you."

He listened carefully. Then his face crumpled, and he started crying.

★

And now here I was, two decades later, driving to pick him up from college. I wondered: *Does Dan have a memory, all these years later, a relic buried deep but almost reachable, of what I told him those long, slow mornings and afternoons? Do he and Zoë know that my attachment to them, so much of the time, was based in fear?*

That fearful attachment was offset by my recurring detachment. I hovered above my family much of the time, observing us from a distance; and as my children grew older, they began to notice when I checked out. They learned to call me back, demanding my attention. "Mom! Mom!"

How much of their childhood did I miss? How much mothering did they miss? When I ask myself these questions, I grieve those day-by-day, year-by-year losses like a death.

I arrived in Cincinnati all tender and melancholy, but Dan broke my mood as soon as he got in the car and slid a Dropkick Murphys CD into the player. We stopped to pick up coffee—when had he started drinking coffee?—and headed north, at which time we proceeded to converse in our usual manner: I interrogated him about school, his roommate, his professors, the food in the cafeteria, his friends, girls, his classes, and the dorm. Dan gave the most circumspect answers he could manage without his lawyer present. Since middle school, he had kept my husband and me on a need-to-know basis, and felt it was entirely reasonable that we didn't need to know anything about him or his life.

I drove on, listening to Dan's CDs and trying hard to like them.

We passed the Five Commandments. Then the next Five Commandments.

After we got through Columbus, we stopped for gas. I was losing my nerve, allowing myself to think I could always tell Dan on the way back to school. There was no deadline on this, after all. But then I thought of Zoë, having to keep it to herself, not talking about it, just the way I had for twenty years.

I had armed myself for this talk by bringing the story that had run in *The Plain Dealer* two days after the rape, a yellowed artifact I'd saved in a hidden folder all those years.

Under the headline, "University Circle rape suspect jailed," the story began: "University Circle police last night arrested a Cleveland man, 27, they believe raped and robbed a Shaker Heights woman at Eldred Hall, the Case Western Reserve University theater."

I gave the paper to him and waited while he read. Then he looked at me, silent and puzzled, not unlike the way he'd looked at me the day of the baby conversation.

Years later, Dan told me he couldn't figure out why I wanted him to read it. He thought maybe I was trying to tell him not to rape women at the University of Cincinnati, but he wasn't sure why I thought he would ever do something like that. It didn't make sense.

When he didn't say anything, I said, "The unnamed Shaker Heights woman in that story was me."

"What?" he said, louder and more emphatic than I had heard him say anything for almost a year. He looked at the story again. "When?"

"It was 1984. A year before you were born."

Silence. He read the story again. I waited. When he finished, he again said nothing.

"I never really knew if I would tell you and Zoë about it," I said. "When you were older, I thought about it a lot, and I decided I had to tell Zoë when I took her to look at colleges. I wanted her to know that this could happen. It could happen to anyone. And if I was going to tell Zoë, I was going to tell you, too."

We both focused on the road ahead of us. In the silence, it occurred to me that I had not felt the need to tell Dan about the rape, or to warn him, before he went to college. I had barely noticed the blue lights on every campus we visited. Why? I wondered. Was I, a feminist, being sexist? Was it because statistics show that 1 in 5 American women are raped in their lifetime, versus 1 in 71 men? Was it because he was six-foot-one and had played varsity hockey all through high school?

"Where is this guy now?" he asked.

"Still in prison, I think. There was a trial and the judge gave him thirty to seventy-five years. It was 1984, so I think that means he can't get out until 2014."

"I hope somebody raped him there," he said. He didn't say anything else.

"Are you OK?" I asked several times. He said yes each time, but nothing more. We didn't talk about it again as we drove home.

Zoë and I talked about it often, though now I remember that I was usually the one to bring it up. When she went to Indiana University, she told me during one phone call that she had talked to some girls in her dorm about my rape.

"They all think it will never happen to them," Zoë said. She was crying.

"That's normal," I said. "If we always thought about the bad things that could happen to us, we'd be too scared to do anything."

My son never again brought it up, and I didn't, either. But a few days later, silent Dan came home with something that spoke for him. He lifted his T-shirt to show me: A heart, like an old-fashioned Valentine with "Mom" on a ribbon inked across it, bloomed on his chest. He had tattooed me on his heart.

It looked like it hurt.

★

I had told my children. I had pulled on the vine, but I knew I had not unearthed it completely. I had to pull on it some more, pull it all the way out, kill it, do something to stop the panic from rising in my chest, stop the *whoosh* of adrenaline that came without warning and made my heart beat so hard you could almost see its movement under my clothes.

I had seen the rapist five times: When he raped me. When I identified him two days later in a lineup. When I sat across a table from him in the county jail three weeks later, to testify in a parole revocation hearing that would keep him in jail. At the trial. And at the sentencing.

I knew he had gone to prison. Beyond that, I didn't know much more than his name. Now it came to me that if I made a list of the most influential people in my life, he would be near the top, with my parents and husband and children.

If it's true that fear grows out of ignorance, which I believe, then maybe I needed to confront the ignorance to get at the fear. I needed to learn more about the man who stood above me and pushed my head toward his penis, the man I thought would be the last human being I would see on this Earth.

The last thing he said to me was, "I will find you," and deep inside the primitive, alarm-prone amygdala at the base of my brain, I still believed him. He had lurked in the shadows of my life all those years, watching me, waiting for me. I still dreamed about him. I still floated out of my body when I thought about him. I thought about him all the time. He was going to find me.

But all I knew was his name—David Francis—his age, that he had lived in Boston at some point, that he had been in prison before, and that he was caught and convicted and sentenced to thirty to seventy-five years in prison.

It occurred to me only much later that I had been sentenced as well, to a mixture of chronic fear, silence, and shame—a shame that never made sense to me, but that I would one day learn I shared with almost all rape victims. Why do we feel this shame? What do we do with it?

After David Francis raped me, I never shook my fists toward the heavens and asked, "Why me?" I knew, or thought I knew, the answer to that one: I was trusting and stupid. But now I wanted the answer to a slightly different question: "Why him?"

We were almost the same age. We both grew up in America in the '60s and '70s. We lived in the same city, just five miles apart. But when my path crossed with his that July day, it brought about a collision of two people who might as well have lived in two different countries. What brought us to that intersection, and what happened to us afterward?

He had been in prison for twenty-one years. He could have been released on parole, but I thought he was probably still locked up. I wondered how prison had changed him, and whether he'd talk to me now. Maybe sitting across from him, with glass between us and guards all around, would make me feel brave, if not fearless.

He'd said he would find me. Maybe I should find him instead.

The familiar dread flooded in when I contemplated this, accompanied by a trembling thought that whispered, *You can't do this. It was a long time ago. He's still in prison. Leave it alone.*

My husband didn't want me to look for him, either.

"He's a monster," he said, not realizing he was echoing the fears that came to me at night. "You don't need to know any more about him than that."

I disagreed. I knew I wouldn't be done with David Francis just by deciding I was. I'd already tried that.

I needed to make sense of my rape. I make sense of things by writing about them. When I was a movie critic, I discovered what I thought about a film through the process of writing about it. Over the years, I had tried this with the rape. I wrote about it, and all that followed it, in an on-again, off-again series of journals I still have. I started and abandoned a novel about it. But this was different.

I hoped writing about David Francis would make the fear go away, but I wanted more. I wanted this random act of rape to have meaning. I wanted to do what human beings have done for thousands of years—tell the stories that help us understand who we are and what happened in our lives to shape us. The way to do it, I figured, was the way I knew best: as a reporter.

In the summer of 2006, not long after Zoë graduated from high school, I started. I wasn't ready to talk to David Francis, not yet, so I began by calling the Cuyahoga County Prosecutor's Office to request the public records in my case. A few days later, they handed over a thick, messy file of police reports, witness statements, rap sheets, subpoenas, lab reports, trial notes, briefs, and indictments, all stuffed together in no particular order and bound with a rubber band.

At home, while sorting the stack into a semblance of order, I came to a page that stopped me.

Across a court record, someone had scrawled the word "DECEASED," and underlined it three times.

David Francis had died in prison on August 18, 2000, sixteen years after he raped me. My search for him was over before I started it.

I sat at my desk with my piles of records, disappointment giving way to relief, relief swinging back to disappointment. I would not get to confront my rapist. On the other hand, I would not have to confront my rapist. The decision had been eliminated for me. David Francis was dead, and so was my story.

The "DECEASED" record sat on top of a large stack of papers. Not knowing what else to do, I started sorting them again, skimming the pages as I went along. I came to his juvenile record from Boston. It had fifty-three entries, detailing crimes and misdemeanors he committed before he turned eighteen. They began when he was twelve.

It occurred to me that while David Francis couldn't talk to me, he still had a lot to tell me. I could follow his path through all these records. I could try to find his family in Boston. Maybe I could find his friends in Cleveland. He had at least a few; I remembered that an alibi witness testified, and lied, for him during his trial. I decided to check the trial transcript to see who she was and what she had to say when she testified.

★

The Old Courthouse opened in 1912, when Cleveland was an industrial powerhouse and the sixth-largest city in the country. It was a town on the go, alive with energy and commerce and immigrants and newcomers, a town many people even now believe could have overshadowed Chicago, with the right leaders and a bit of luck.

The courthouse was one of the public buildings the city leaders envisioned in 1903, when they commissioned a grand civic plan to echo the mall in Washington, D.C. The plan, which grew out of the City Beautiful Movement, called for a formal grouping of Beaux Arts–style buildings around a broad, grassy mall that led to a vista of Lake Erie.

The second building to go up, the courthouse was intended to inspire awe among the citizens who entered it seeking justice. A hundred years later it still does a pretty good job of it. Life-size bronze statues of Thomas Jefferson and Alexander Hamilton flank the wide stairs leading to the front entrance. Above them, on a ledge surrounding the building, stand statues of the great lawgivers of history, from Moses on. Inside, twin marble staircases curl up the three-story marble rotunda, where a stained-glass window of Lady Justice looks down from a perch positioned to catch the rising sun.

Eventually the county outgrew the courthouse, and in 1976 most court operations moved to the ugly new Justice Center tower across the street. The graceful Old Courthouse remained open, though, home to the domestic relations and probate courts, where the people of Cuyahoga County go to get their marriage licenses and, later, their divorces, and where they go to deal with death.

The grand staircase led me down to the basement, a dim warren of offices and storage rooms. A canteen near the stairs sells tepid coffee and off-brand packaged snacks, and every time I went there I passed divorce lawyers huddled at the wobbly tables with their clients, most of them weeping.

In this basement, the county's Clerk of Courts keeps all of its millions of pages of transcripts and criminal evidence. In 2006, when I first went there, none of the records were digital, and the archives of documents overwhelmed the space allotted.

In the hallways, towers of stacked file boxes along the walls formed a cardboard canyon of mortgage foreclosures, divorce actions, child-custody battles, competency hearings, property disputes, robbery trials, murder trials, rape trials. These were the records that would not fit in the overstuffed file rooms, where more boxes were stacked to the water-damaged ceilings.

As I walked through the canyon of files, I felt like a visitor to the Catacombs of Paris, wandering through tunnels lined with skulls and bones. I had entered an ancient repository of grief, a place that held the memories of the collective pain, bitterness, fear, and sorrow of the people of Cuyahoga County. My small piece of it came in the file of Case Number CR-193108: *The State of Ohio v. David Francis.*

I filled out a printed form and handed it to a clerk in a crowded office at the end of the hall. He returned a few minutes later carrying two expandable dark red envelopes stuffed with files, each held together with a rubber band. He gestured toward a table in the hallway and said, "Don't take these out of this area." That warning was the extent of the court's security system.

I opened the smaller envelope. Out tumbled the evidence from my trial: a gold cross on a chain, a dozen Polaroids, some mug shots, and two tiny glassine envelopes containing pubic hair samples, mine and the rapist's. I had forgotten about the embarrassing collection of the hair. I put the envelopes back with my fingernails, as carefully as if they contained anthrax.

The Polaroids showed my body, most without my head. Two of them showed my back, an abstract design of red lacerations and bruises turning blue and purple. Others showed a small red gash on my neck and puncture wounds on my fingers. I studied them. The photos looked like porn for a scar fetishist. They were crude shots of a body without the woman inhabiting it, a portrait of everything the rape did to me. I slid them back into the envelope.

The second one, much thicker, held the trial transcript.

On the first page, I read: *Be it remembered, that at the September, 1984 term of said court, to-wit, commencing on Wednesday, the 17th day of October, this cause came on to be heard . . .*

I trembled, surprising myself.

Be it remembered.

I turned to my testimony. There, on the onionskin pages, I found the Joanna of twenty-two years before. She was trembling, too, I remembered, as she told the jury what happened that day.

CHAPTER TWO

"If I have to go to prison, I'll miss you"

Monday, July 9, 1984. Cleveland.

On the last day of the first part of my life, I'm running late. As usual.

Damn it, damn it, damn it.

I'm driving up Euclid Avenue in my Toyota hatchback, fifteen miles an hour over the speed limit, pushing it to twenty, headed east out of downtown Cleveland for a 5:00 p.m. interview at Case Western Reserve University.

It's already 5:00. Rush hour starts at 4:30 here, and I'm trapped in the daily exodus of workers leaving their offices in the city for the suburbs, all of them stepping on the gas through the bad parts of town, speeding past the brick housing projects and the weedy vacant lots that mark the spots where riots burned through in the '60s.

At East 55th Street, the borderline between downtown and the inner city, you can almost hear the steady beat of car locks clicking down, the percussive sound track to Cleveland's deep racial divide.

I slalom from the left lane to the right lane and back, swearing and scolding myself the way I always do.

Why don't you leave more time? Jesus. What's wrong with you?

It's high summer, and I'm worked up and jittery, hitting the steering wheel as I talk. The car has no air-conditioning. My open window lets in the heavy, hot fumes of summer, melting tar and truck diesel. All I want to do is get to Case, do a quick interview, and then head to my neighborhood pool for an evening swim before it closes. I'm thinking more about the pool than the interview, which I'm doing only because the guy who runs the little summer theater on the Case campus bugged me so much about it. I've agreed to watch a rehearsal of their next show, and then talk to the playwright, someone I've never heard of, who's in from Peru. I've been so busy I haven't read the play or anything about the playwright. I'll wing it.

At this point, I've lived in Cleveland only ten months. I still get lost, still don't know all the shortcuts. I keep up the yelling at myself and other drivers as I head into the rush-hour snarl of University Circle, a hub of culture, education, and verdant parks at the eastern edge of the city. The Circle is the rose on the lapel of Cleveland's threadbare jacket, financed by the likes of John D. Rockefeller and the city's other titans of the Gilded Age as the home to the Cleveland Orchestra, the Cleveland Museum of Art, two history museums, a botanical garden, art and music schools, and Case Western Reserve University.

On the many occasions when our civic dignity is wounded, Clevelanders always invoke University Circle to restore our pride.

It's no easy task. Magazines continually put us on soul-crushing lists, naming us the fattest city in America, or the poorest, or the least sexy, or—the latest—the most miserable city in America. I like to imagine teams of statisticians with clipboards going door to door, measuring the misery of an entire city, offering tissues and hugs as they listen.

I forget how this one determined misery. The choices are many, topped by dreary winter weather, high unemployment, and the sorry history of our teams. Cleveland still has three major-league teams, but they all lose so often, and so spectacularly, that my newspaper calls it a "streak" if any of them win two games in a row. The nickname for the stadium where the Cleveland Browns play is "The Factory of Sadness." After LeBron James took his talents to South Beach, ESPN found few reasons to even mention Cleveland, and resumed paying attention only when he came back in 2014. Before the first home game after LeBron returned, Clevelanders filled the streets downtown, the mass celebration reaching a level of joy and mayhem that other cities might reserve for a World Series or Super Bowl win.

The Cavaliers lost the game.

After delivering that familiar disappointment, the team then astonished everyone in Cleveland by starting to win, making it to the playoffs, winning again, and continuing to the NBA Championship Finals. Which they lost.

Clevelanders, their hopes crushed yet again, immediately started talking about next year.

On one border of University Circle you have the massive Cleveland Clinic, a Legoland where new buildings appear

almost overnight, usually followed by squat bodyguards outfitted with Secret Service–style earpieces, there to protect the
Middle Eastern shahs and princesses who jet into Cleveland
for luxe treatment on private hospital floors. A few years back,
a rumor circulated that one shah arrived with his own "volunteer" kidney donor in tow. Some said it was because he did not
want to wait on an official donor list; others said it was simply
a matter of not trusting the quality of our kidneys.

A couple of blocks from the clinic is Hough, the poor,
predominantly black neighborhood where a six-day riot,
sparked by racial tensions between black residents and the
police and white business owners, broke out in 1966, the
middle of the decade of urban riots in America. Four people
died. Two years later, in Glenville, another neighborhood
that borders University Circle, a shoot-out between black
nationalists and Cleveland police sparked a three-day riot
that left seven people dead.

When we moved to Cleveland from Minneapolis in the
summer of 1983, we knew little of this. Most of what my
husband and I knew of the city fit on the invitation to our
going-away party, which featured a picture of that burning
Cuyahoga River and a woman from a '50s horror movie
running away in terror. "Cleveland, City of Light, City of
Magic," it said, adopting Randy Newman's ironic ode to our
new home.

None of our friends could imagine why we would move
to a city that was a punch line for late-night comedians: *First
prize: A week in Cleveland! Second prize: Two weeks in Cleveland!
Ba-da-bum.* The city offered so much material for mockery.

The burning river. The stinky steel mills. The mayor who set his hair on fire with a blowtorch when he cut a ceremonial metal ribbon to open a convention. The wife of that same mayor, who declined an invitation to the Nixon White House because it was her bowling night. (It was, in her defense, the league championship.)

Our reason was simple and embarrassing: We moved to Cleveland because we had quit our jobs at the *Minneapolis Star* on impulse, in a buyout, and *The Plain Dealer* was the first paper to offer us both employment. We were twenty-nine. We decided we would stay five years, then move on.

That summer of 1983 was the summer of *Return of the Jedi*, which supposedly completed the Star Wars trilogy but did not. Madonna released her first album. Michael Jackson introduced the Moonwalk. WMMS was the hot radio station in Cleveland, playing "Every Breath You Take" and "Beat It" in constant rotation. That summer, *Scientific American* reported that crack cocaine, which in 1983 was just beginning to creep onto the streets of big cities like Cleveland, was "as addictive as potato chips."

In Cleveland, it was also the summer of the smash-and-grab. That was the first thing everyone warned me about when they discovered I was new to town. "Don't leave your windows open or your purse on the passenger seat," they said, over and over again, those first months. "At stoplights, they smash the window and grab it before you even know what's happening."

"They," while never overtly identified, implied the black men and boys in the designated danger zones of the city—Hough,

Central, Fairfax, Glenville: neighborhoods that still showed the scars of the riots in 1966 and 1968. Block after block was pocked with weedy vacant lots and houses with windows covered in plywood and graffiti, where people slipped in and out of the back doors like shadows. Many of them came from the suburbs. In 1990, the celebrated, and winning, and white, coach of the Cleveland State University basketball team was one of those shadows, caught leaving a crack house with a prostitute on his arm.

Hough, once a fashionable neighborhood of three-story houses with wide front porches, changed in the space of a single decade, going from 95 percent white in 1950 to 74 percent black in 1960. Urban renewal and the last gasp of the great migration from the South pushed black people out of the central city and into Hough. Realtors lit the flame of panic selling and white flight to the suburbs up the hill, Shaker Heights and Cleveland Heights.

By the summer of 1983, Hough was a place I was told you did not go if you were white. Of course, black people had danger zones, too. They were warned not to go to Little Italy, where the aging vestiges of the Cleveland Mafia passed the day drinking espresso at sidewalk cafés and young white men attacked black people who dared cross into their territory.

You drove through Hough, along Chester or Superior Avenue, to get from the suburbs to downtown. But you didn't turn onto the side streets. Or so I was told. My husband, working the police beat that first year, told me not to stop at red lights if I ever came home late at night.

Sometimes that first year I felt like a child listening to fairy tales about the dangers lurking in the woods. Go straight to work, Little Red Riding Hood, and don't stop or the wolf might get you.

What did I know? I had lived in Minneapolis–St. Paul for a decade, where the black population appeared to consist of Prince and about a dozen other people. A black reporter who had recently arrived from Texas came into the newsroom one day and said she'd spotted some black people on the street and followed them in her car, hoping to find out where all the black folks lived. She left after a year. "This place is just too white," she said as she departed.

In Cleveland, smash-and-grabs turned out to be the least of the dire warnings. When I went to look at an apartment in Cleveland Heights, the landlord warned me of an epidemic of carjackings. As we stood in the living room, the sun slanting on the polished wood floors, he told me that one of the women in the building had just bought a BMW, and I should think about it, too.

"She used to have a Mercedes," he said, "but that's one of the cars they like to take. A little dangerous for a woman to drive. BMWs are just as good a car, but they're not as flashy."

He clearly had no idea where newspaper reporters lined up on the pay scale.

★

Monday, July 9, 1984.

It's 5:15 p.m. when I pull into the parking lot at Case. I run to Eldred Theater, stumbling a little in the heels and linen skirt I put on that morning to look professional. The doors into the building are open when I get there. *Maybe they're still rehearsing and haven't even noticed I'm late.* I run up the stairs to the small lobby area on the second floor and look into the theater.

Empty. The whole place is empty.

Damn it! They're gone.

I must have said it out loud, because a voice comes out of the shadows across the landing. "They said to wait a few minutes. They'll be back."

The guy who said it is leaning against the wall, smoking. He's wiry, not much bigger than me, with an Afro and plastic-framed glasses the size of salad plates, just like mine. It's the '80s, the decade of the Giant Glasses.

"They did?" I say. "Oh."

I wait, sticking to my side of the little lobby. I feel awkward, like I should say something else, but he's not saying anything, either. I think about asking him for a cigarette, even though I don't really smoke. I used to, starting when I was a freshman in high school, and hid my cigarettes in a metal Band-Aid box, right up until I was twenty-two and my chain-smoking father died of a heart attack at the age of forty-seven. The day after his funeral I quit, though I still bummed cigarettes when I was in a bar or around other people smoking.

I'm about to ask the guy for one when I smell menthol in the smoke curling across the lobby. Forget it. I hate menthol.

A couple of minutes pass. He stubs out his cigarette on the floor, shakes another from his pack. Kools.

As he lights it, I decide I'm done waiting and turn to go back down the stairs.

"I'm working on the lights," he says to my back, his voice mild. "Do you want to see what I've been doing?"

A yellow light flashes briefly in my head: *Caution. You don't know this guy.*

I ignore it. It's just a flash, and I speed through it the same way I'd sped through every yellow light on Euclid Avenue driving here.

"OK," I say.

The door to the theater is closed.

I open it and walk through, into the dark theater and the second part of my life.

I make my way down the narrow right aisle and climb the two steps to the stage, the guy right behind me.

I turn and look up at the stage lights. They're off. Only the house lights are on. He says, "I should turn them on." He doesn't move.

Animal alarm flashes through my body, followed by a flood of adrenaline. The surge makes me dizzy.

This is not right, I think. *In fact, this is bad. Really bad. Get out of here. Now.*

"I think I'll wait outside," I say. Still polite. Still the good girl.

I know it's too late in the second before he grabs me from behind, pinning my arms to my sides.

I try to scream. I want to scream. It should be natural: Danger leads to fear leads to scream.

But my body has other ideas. Panic overtakes me and closes my throat into a tight, burning knot, muting me. All I can manage is a strangled, small, "No," just above a whisper.

"Be quiet," he says.

I feel metal on my neck, moving slowly under my jawline. A sharp point presses into the skin.

I stop moving, stop trying to scream. My attention focuses on that one small point of cool metal against my throbbing vein.

He has a knife. He has a knife. The thought pulses with my blood, a hundred beats a second.

"Please don't do this," I say. "Do you want money? Do you want my purse? Take anything you want, but please don't hurt me."

"Now, just be quiet," he says, his voice calm, soothing, as though I'm a child who just woke up from a nightmare.

He pushes me behind the scrim, a translucent screen at the very back of the stage, then backs me hard against the concrete wall, his hand to my mouth. He shows me the knife. It isn't a knife, though: It's half a pair of long utility scissors, the kind with black handles and a sharp point. A makeshift dagger.

"Now, I can kill you," he says, still calm, like he's saying he can get me a cup of coffee. "But I won't kill you if you do what I say."

My breath stops. Wait. *Kill me?*

The world shrinks into the small, still space behind the scrim. Nothing else exists.

★

How did this happen? One minute I was running toward a college theater, thinking about how I would fake my way through the interview, get to the pool, and then figure out something for dinner. The ordinary middle of an ordinary day of my ordinary life.

I catch a flash of steel when he moves his hand. An image appears, unbidden: my mother cutting fabric on our dining room table, pins held between her lips, her long, black-handled utility scissors crinkling the tissue-paper patterns of dresses.

His hand still covers my mouth. I nod: Yes. I will do what he tells me.

He takes his hand from my mouth. I do not say anything as he starts fumbling with the buttons on my blouse.

I shake. I try to stop it, but I can't.

This is it. My rape. I knew it was coming. Every woman knows it, anticipates it, fears it, yet also doesn't believe it will happen to her. And now here it is. My turn.

My stomach drops, but I do not let myself cry. The effort burns my throat.

I think of something that might stop him. "I'm having my period," I say. I try to sound apologetic.

"Be quiet."

He tears at the last button on my blouse, and as he pulls it off I see drops of blood dotting the front.

My mind takes a few seconds to catch up to this new piece of information.

My blood?

I put my hand to my neck, where the dagger was. Sticky. I look at my hand. A bright red smear.

Yes. My blood.

I look down and see more blood on my skirt. My new linen skirt, bought to celebrate the new job. Bought to look professional.

As though it recognizes itself, the blood in my veins springs to action. I feel it pounding upward, squeezing through my carotid artery, pushing into my head. My body is electrical wire, the current switched on.

Then, just as suddenly, it turns off.

I slip away from my body, like Peter Pan's shadow, into the fly space above the stage. My fear has vanished. I look down at the stage. I see myself. I look small, standing there in my bra. I look scared.

From the moment we humans are shocked with the terrible knowledge of our own mortality, we wonder and fear: *How will I die? When will I die?*

A guy smoking a Kool just delivered my answer.

Now.

Now is when it happens to me.

★

I don't find it strange that there are two of me. On the stage, I feel his hands on my body. I feel the blade next to my neck, then next to my chest. I feel the rough concrete wall scrape at the skin on my back.

From up above, I watch all of this with a soothing detachment. I know it's me down there, but I feel like I'm watching someone else. A girl in a play. For her, I feel . . . I guess the word is "concern." And pity.

Down on the stage, my blouse is on the ground. My skirt lies in a puddle at my feet. He fumbles with his zipper, still trying to hold the scissors at my neck. He tells me to take off my shoes and everything else.

It occurs to me—probably not then, probably later—that rape is a clumsy business. It's nothing like the movie versions. The clothes come right off in the movies, usually ripped dramatically. Nothing gets stuck. The rapist knows what he's doing and works with efficiency. He never has trouble maintaining an erection. As for the victim, she either fights back and escapes—after kneeing the rapist in the groin, of course—or she dies in horrifying violence that will be avenged by the hero.

I, on the other hand, almost topple over while I unbuckle my shoes. My underwear binds my ankles. The rapist still can't get his zipper down.

Up above, I decide he really is not the right person for the role of rapist. Not at all. He's too young, too skinny, barely taller than me. His mesh tank top is the kind favored by men who spend a lot of time in the gym, but he has no muscles to show off, no pecs rippling under the shiny mesh. No, he isn't right for the role. Not scary enough. He will be something of a disappointment to the audience.

The rapist finally gets his zipper to work and sheds his pants, revealing gray boxers. I wonder idly from above: *Are they gray because he never washes them, or is that their original color? I hope, for the girl's sake, it's the latter.*

He shoves me against the concrete wall and tries to push his penis into me, standing up. But he's not tall enough, and his penis isn't hard enough. He turns me around and tries again from the back. The concrete feels cold on my cheek.

When standing doesn't work, he pushes me down to my hands and knees, kneels behind me. He forces a finger into my vagina, as if trying to locate it, and then presses his semisoft penis into me and starts thrusting. Fast. Faster. He's pumping away so fast I think it will end quickly, but after a couple of minutes he gets tired, or bored, turns me over onto my back on the stage floor, and pushes his penis into me again, from the front.

He moves with mechanical disinterest, not speaking, not looking down at me. Above, watching, I wonder if he even feels excited. As he continues to thrust, grunting, a small cross hanging from his neck dangles in my face. Lying under him, I fix my eyes on it as it swings, back and forth, a hypnotist's charm.

He stops, abruptly, and looks me in the eye.

"Are you married?"

I hesitate.

Is this a test? What answer does he want?

Then I realize he must have seen my wedding ring.

"Yes," I say. Nothing more.

"Have you ever had a black man before?"

Now what should I say? Does he care?

"No." A lie. I had two black boyfriends in college.

"I bet you've always wanted to," he says. He leans close, his breath hot with the smell of cigarettes and alcohol. This time, I know what he wants me to answer.

"Yes," I say.

He stands and pulls me up by my hair, then pushes me to my knees.

"I got to get off," he says, and presses my face to his groin, still holding my hair.

"Suck on it," he says.

His penis has gone soft again. I look at it, nestled like a small bird in the coarse black hair. I close my eyes and take it in my mouth. Smell and taste hit me at once. Urine. Sweat. Something musky and rank. I gag and try to cover the gag.

Up above, watching, I wait for the girl on the stage to bite the penis. That's what they do in movies. They bite it. They hit the guy in the balls. They scream. They scratch. They escape.

The girl onstage does not bite. She sucks. He stays soft.

"Harder," he says.

She sucks harder. She can't breathe. She keeps going.

Up above, I observe: This is pathetic. Pathetic rapist. Pathetic blow job. If the girl were better at it, this would be over. She can't even make a rapist come.

He grabs me by the hair and pulls me away from his penis. "Lie down," he says. I do, lying on a strip of red carpet embedded with the grime of years of entrances and exits.

★

Time passes and stops at the same time. I do everything the rapist tells me to do. I suck. I lie down. I turn over. He directs me in an automated, perfunctory Kama Sutra.

I understand that the only way this will end is for him to come, so I try to excite him. I move my hips, I thrust back, I kneel in submission. I make noises of pleasure. *Oooohh. Mmmmm.* I kiss him back.

"Do you like this?" he asks. Three, four times he asks.

"Yes," I say.

Nothing I do matters. Even as he moves me around, muttering, "I got to get off," he seems oddly bored by what he is doing.

He loses his soft erection and turns me over yet again, pulls my bottom up and jabs a finger in.

"Have you ever been fucked in the ass?" he asks.

He doesn't wait for an answer. This excites him. His penis hard, he sodomizes me, pushing in fast and without warning.

The pain stuns me. It burns. I fight for air. My face, rubbing into the dirty backstage carpet, is wet and raw. I have held back my tears, but now I choke on them.

"Does your husband do this?" he asks.

I close my eyes and try to breathe.

"Does it feel good?"

He coos the words into my ear. He's hurting me; he has to know he's hurting me. Dirt and carpet fibers catch in my throat. I hold my breath and try to give in to the pain, to make it go away.

"Does it feel good?" he asks again.

"Yes."

"Does your husband do this to you?"

Then it hits me.

This is a prison rape.

Of course. He's been in prison, and now he's doing to me what someone did to him. He's claiming me as his property.

Then: A noise from downstairs. A bang, like a door closing.

Bang: *Someone is here.* Bang: *I will be rescued.* Bang: *No. He'll panic and stab me.*

He stops, puts his hand over my mouth, and grabs the weapon, pulling out but still hovering over me.

"Be quiet, now. Be quiet." I nod and he takes his hand away. We freeze in place.

Silence.

Silence.

Nothing.

No one is coming. I won't be rescued. He will kill me.

He pushes me to the floor again, and keeps going, posing me like a doll: on my back, on my hands and knees, on my stomach. Then he put his penis in my mouth again, hovering above my face as I lie there. I gag, bile rising in a bitter gush into my throat. I can't breathe. The penis falls away from my mouth.

He slaps my face. "Bitch."

Then he caresses the spot where he slapped. Gentle.

"You're my bitch," he says. "You do what I tell you."

He moves down my body and burrows his face between my legs. He licks.

Above, I observe: This is weird. Rapists don't do this. Do they?

He licks more.

Up above, I decide he really doesn't know what he's doing. I want to shout down at him: *God! Have you ever done this before?*

He stops. "I know you liked that," he says, pride in his voice, as he climbs on top of me again.

How long has it been? I have no idea. The theater feels like a sealed tomb, something out of an Edgar Allan Poe story, soundproof and windowless, with a trapped heart beating inside. I am alone. Utterly alone.

I watch from above. How will it end?

I try something: "I think the people I was supposed to meet will come back," I say. "They might catch us. We should get out of here."

He looks at me, thinking about it. Then he nods and reaches for his pants. I crawl across the dirty carpet for my skirt. We dress in a hurry.

"Get your purse," he says.

I give him all my money: a couple of twenties and some singles. He grabs the wallet from my hands and shakes the coins out, pocketing the quarters and dimes and pennies.

When he has everything, he puts the dagger-scissors up to my back and pushes the point in just enough so I can feel it.

"OK," he says. "We're going to go outside now. I told you I wouldn't kill you, but if you do anything stupid when we get out, I will kill you."

He leads me out a backstage door and down a staircase, holding my arm, the point of the scissors pressing into my back.

Then he opens a door and we are outside. My brain registers the change in one-word thoughts: *Bright. Sun. Air.*

Then: *DAVE.*

In the sun, I see a tattoo on his right arm: *"DAVE,"* carved into his dark skin in crude capital letters. It looks like someone etched it with a sharpened ballpoint pen. *Or scissors,* I think, feeling the point in my back.

I glance at him and look away. Now I know his face and his name, or maybe his prison boyfriend's name. Did he notice that I saw it?

"Where's your car?" he asks.

My tiny flame of hope sputters and dies. I'm outside, but I'm not free. And now I know too much for him to let me go. Now he'll take me somewhere in my car and kill me. I hesitate.

"It's in the lot over there," I say. Then I add: "Right next to the attendant's booth."

This is not true, but I continue the lie. "We can't go there. We don't want to get caught."

He thinks for a second, then turns me so I'm facing him. He licks his finger and rubs at the blood on my neck. He smooths my hair.

"Now, don't you go to the cops," he says. "If you go to the cops, I'll have to go to prison."

"I won't go to the cops. I promise."

"If I have to go to prison, I'll miss you," he says, almost cooing. "And when I get out, I will find you."

He kisses me on the lips and walks away.

CHAPTER THREE

I want this written on my body

I wobble toward my car, holding my torn blouse closed with one hand, the straps on my shoes flapping with each step.

The midsummer evening feels like afternoon, bright and hot, the burned smell of asphalt rising in the still air. The paths through the campus are empty. Everyone has gone home, which is where I'm supposed to be by now. I hear traffic a block away, the hum of the last gasp of rush hour, people thinking about dinner and wondering what's on TV tonight.

When I get to the parking lot, I see someone in the booth. A man in a uniform. I stumble across the tarmac toward him. He will make me safe.

When he slides the window open, I stand there, mute. My throat clamps shut again. He notices my ripped blouse.

I blurt out, "I was just raped."

It's the first time I say the words, and it sounds wrong. Too flat. Too direct. I feel like a fake, a feeling that will return again and again in the days and weeks to come. Why am I not crying or wailing like a real victim? Why do I sound so emotionless? After stating just the fact, I am unable to say anything else.

The man in the booth doesn't know what to say, either. He falters for a few seconds, staring at me, and then opens the door and points to his stool. "Sit here." He looks like someone's grandfather. I feel bad for him, having to deal with this. I sit on his stool, shaking, while he talks into a walkie-talkie. "I have a rape victim here," he says, and then he steps outside of the booth to wait, leaving me alone for the first time that night.

Seconds later, a guy in a red pickup pulls up and shouts into the window, "Which way did he go?" I point toward Euclid Avenue and the guy speeds off, and before I can figure out how he knew about the rape, a cop car pulls up, and I'm out of the booth and in the front seat.

The cop does not want the story. He wants a description: What was his race? What did he look like? How tall was he? What was his weight?

"Black," I say. "But I'm not sure how tall he was. I'm not sure about his weight, either. It's hard to estimate."

The cop tries to help: "Was he taller than you, or shorter? Heavier?"

"A little taller than me. He was pretty thin, so I'm not sure if he was heavier."

"How much do you weigh?"

I pause. "About one thirty," I say, automatically shaving off the traditional five pounds. This will worry me quite a bit later on. Will someone discover I lied about my weight, and so must be lying about everything else, too?

After more back-and-forth, we arrive at a description: Wiry build, maybe a hundred forty pounds. Slightly taller than me. I'm five-six, so maybe five-seven or five-eight.

"What about his color," the cop says. "Was he dark or light-skinned?" Again I hesitate. I've never described the gradations of African-American skin color; I don't know the benchmarks.

"I guess he was light," I say. "Maybe he was medium. I don't know."

I try to make up for my indecisiveness by offering something better: "He had a tattoo. A name tattooed on his right bicep. 'DAVE.' It was all in capital letters, and messy, like it was made with a pen or a knife." The cop nods with approval. I have a moment where I feel like what I always tried to be as a child: I'm a good girl.

Then we are at the emergency room, where a dozen people slump in rows of plastic chairs, waiting for someone to see them. The room is dim. A TV hung on the wall plays without sound.

The cop rushes me through the waiting room like a celebrity he has to protect from overzealous fans. If I had a coat, he probably would drape it over my head. He tells me the Cleveland police will come to talk to me. He tells me I did a good job with the description. Then he leaves.

Inside the ER, the intake nurse puts me in a private room, one with a door instead of curtains. With brisk efficiency, she hands me a paper gown and asks for my clothes, then stuffs them into a bag to give to the police. Evidence, she tells me.

She brings me a cup of water. She takes down all my information, my history. She asks me who she should call to come to the hospital for me. Am I married? I give her my husband's phone number at work. She tells me the doctor will be there soon, but first the police need to talk to me. A hospital social worker will come by, too. Do I want someone from the Rape Crisis Center to come? Yes. Please. Then she leaves.

I am alone.

A clock on the wall ticks the seconds. It's past 6:30. I thought it would be later. Time, after disappearing in that theater, returns to me. It lasted an hour. DAVE trapped me and raped me for an hour.

Outside the room, a gurney rolls past, clacking. Someone moans, then moans louder. Two people rush past my door. I hear the word "gunshot."

I am alone.

I am afraid.

The air conditioner vent above me blasts refrigerated air into the room. I sit on the exam table in the paper gown, wishing the nurse had given me a blanket. I think again of the other girls, the ones who did not make it to the ER, lying cold in a wooded area off a highway—it always seemed to be just off the highway—under a layer of dirt and brush, waiting for someone to stumble over them.

After a while, I lie back on the table, the paper crinkling under my body, my hands cradling my head. In the silent, chilled room, naked under the gown, I feel like a forgotten corpse, awaiting my own autopsy.

My hand goes to my neck, where he cut me. It's stopped bleeding. I can feel now that the cut is small, a couple of inches long, maybe three. It is not deep. It is nothing much. I worry about this: *Maybe I don't look hurt. Maybe the cut is so minimal, the doctor will not believe me. The cops won't believe me.*

I start crying. I want the wound to be bigger. I want it deeper. I want it to hurt. I want them to gasp when they see it, the doctors and cops, I want them to ask me how I managed to survive. I want them to tell me they are calling in the top plastic surgeon to stitch it up, so I will not have a scar.

I want this written on my body. Tattooed on my body.

I stop crying and drift, lying on the table. Then they come in, one by one. First the hospital social worker. Then a Cleveland policeman in uniform. Then another nurse. Then the Rape Crisis Center volunteer.

They ask me what happened. The rape crisis volunteer holds my hand while I talk. One by one, I tell them. But what I tell is not my story, it is a list: He did this, then he did that. He was wearing this. He looked like this. He said this. I was scared. I cried. I did what he told me to do.

I do not tell them that I left my body.

They nod, write it all down. "Then what happened?" they all ask. I continue the list.

I know I should be sobbing, shaking, screaming, not reciting a list in a monotone. When I get to the part about the anal rape, the cop goes still. He looks away from me.

With each interview, I leave out the most important fact of all: It was my fault. My own, stupid, gullible, naïve fault. I was late. I walked into that empty theater. I ignored my own warning light. I practically invited DAVE to rape me.

The cops give me their cards. The Rape Crisis Center volunteer gives me a card with phone numbers to call the next day. Then they leave me alone in the room again. Time passes.

The nurse returns with the doctor, a resident who looks like she might be on her twenty-sixth hour of duty, rushing from patient to patient. She gets right to business, her jaws working hard on a wad of bubble gum while she reads my chart. When she bends toward me to look at the cut on my neck, her breath smells like cotton candy.

I note that she does not gasp at the cut. She cleans it with something that smells like alcohol, then asks me if I am OK with her examining me. She says she needs to prepare a rape kit to give to the police—she has a legal protocol to follow.

The stirrups are cold. When I shiver, she warns me that the metal speculum might be cold, too. She inserts it and swabs and scrapes inside me, handing each instrument and swab to the nurse, explaining to me every step of the procedure as she works. She tells me she's combing my public hair for his hair, swabbing for semen, looking for signs of trauma, gathering evidence of the rape in the folds and secretions inside me. She swabs inside my anus.

"Basically, your body is the main piece of evidence here," she says as she works, chewing her gum.

My other self, hovering above, looks down at me, lying on the table with my feet in stirrups, my hands cradling my head.

Still too calm, I think.

CHAPTER FOUR

She's gone

The nurse calls my husband, but only tells him I'm in the ER, that I was in an accident and that I'm OK. They leave it to me to tell him what happened.

I am alone yet again in the ER room, lying on the exam table, looking at the ceiling, when the nurse brings him in. I sit up. The nurse almost tiptoes out.

"What happened?" He looks and sounds panicked.

I feel weird that I'm not crying, but I cannot produce tears. After all my panic, I feel numb.

"I," I say, and stop. I can't utter the words. I said them to the parking lot attendant, to the cops and social worker and nurse and doctor. But I do not want to say them to my husband. Why didn't the nurse tell him, or the cops? Are the cops gone?

"I . . ."

Now I'm standing. He hugs me. My throat burns and clutches up, the way it did when the rapist grabbed me from behind.

"I was raped." I whisper it into his shoulder.

"Oh no." He hugs me tighter. "Are you OK?"

I am alive. But I don't think I'm OK. I won't know if I am for a long time. Years.

There in the ER, two hours after I was raped, I begin what will become my pattern with everyone close to me: I reassure him. Instead of crying, "No, I'm not OK!" and asking for his help, I speed past my own needs and arrive at his. He needs me to be OK.

"Yes," I say. "I'm OK."

It's dark by the time they finish with me. They give me green scrubs with drawstring pants to wear home. Walking to my husband's car in the oversized scrubs and my high heels, I still feel watched. I'm still performing in a movie about a young woman, much like me, who has been raped.

We don't talk as my husband drives home, to the house in Shaker Heights we just bought. I haven't put up curtains yet, or laid rugs on the hardwood floors, or unpacked all the boxes. The house is dark when we pull in. When we open the back door, it feels like we're breaking in. In the stillness, my husband whispers that he will run a bath for me.

I don't want a bath, I want a shower, hot and hotter still, to scald my skin. I say nothing and step into the tub, easing my body into the warm water. I close my eyes and lean back. When I don't say anything, he goes downstairs.

I am alone.

I don't want to be alone. But I don't want to talk, either. I want to be comforted, but I don't want to hug or touch. I hear him in the kitchen, opening cabinets. I scrub myself with a washcloth and sit in the water as it grows cold.

He makes dinner for me. Broiled shrimp. I take a couple of bites, like a polite dinner guest, washing the faintly metallic taste out with a cold beer. When we finish, we climb the stairs to our bedroom. I tell him I can't call my sisters or my mother. My excuse is that I'm too tired. I've already told too many people.

He doesn't know what to do, or how to ask me if he can touch me. I get into bed and tell him to get in, too. I hug him in bed. Then he holds me, spooned against my back.

When the tidal rhythm of his breathing tells me he's asleep, I inch away from him. I move to the edge of the bed, curling into myself like one of those insects that rolls into a tight ball when it senses danger.

I lie awake, listening to the rhythmic counterpoint of my husband's breath and the chirping sounds of the summer night.

Safe. Here I am supposed to be safe. But I can't believe it anymore. I've lost the illusion, the pretty, dangerous illusion, that the world is safe. The woman who woke up in this bed fourteen hours ago—the woman who was five minutes late to everything, the woman who thought bad things happened to other people, if she thought about it at all—is gone.

CHAPTER FIVE

The Wino

Tuesday, July 10, 1984.

The next day, DAVE does something no one can quite believe.

He returns to the scene of the crime. Not only that, he returns at the same time of day, wearing the same clothes. He must have believed me when I said I wouldn't go to the cops. Maybe he even thought I'd come back.

At 4:53 p.m., he saunters into the quad near Eldred Theater, walking north, past a wino sitting on a bench with his bottle in a paper bag. He passes a small waterfall sculpture. The wino watches him, but DAVE doesn't notice. He stops at a bench, sits down. Across the quad, the wino takes a drink. After a minute or two, DAVE gets up and walks west, toward Severance Hall. The wino follows him from a distance. He lifts his paper bag to his mouth again.

Up ahead, a University Circle patrol car pulls into a lot. DAVE sees it and changes direction, heading east toward the hospital, where two hospital security guards stop him. Within a minute, three University Circle cops converge.

The wino arrives next, still carrying his bag. He notes that DAVE's zipper is open.

★

I did not know the wino story until I read the trial transcript in 2007.

The wino testified on the third day of the trial in October of 1984. His name was Larry Donovan, and he was an investigator for the University Circle Police Department, a security force created for and paid by Case Western and all the other institutions in University Circle. I had met him, briefly, outside of court when he came to testify during the trial, but I was sequestered outside the courtroom and didn't hear his testimony.

When we met for coffee in 2007, I almost didn't recognize him. He still had the big Irish smile and ruddy cheeks I remembered, but he was much heavier than he had been back in 1984 and he limped, a state of affairs he blamed on a bum knee. He told me he had gone back to school not long after the arrest to get a degree in engineering while still working as a cop. He worked in computer technology for a while and then went to law school. Now he practices intellectual property law, where a background in engineering is useful.

I asked him if he remembered the case.

"Oh yeah," he said. "That was a big one for us. We were all proud of how it came out."

Even then, so many years later, I was pleased to hear that the case was a big one for them, that this cop remembered it. I thought of the cut on my neck. I wanted it to be big, I wanted it to leave a scar, and I was disappointed when it was small and didn't show. Yet back then, within days I had minimized my rape, insisting that I was fine and denying, even to myself, that I had been wounded in other ways, and that the wound was deep. I made sure no one could accuse me of the grave feminine sins of self-pity and victim-playing. Now that a cop—a man familiar with violence—said it was big, maybe I could admit it to myself.

"Who came up with the wino disguise?" I asked.

"That was mine," he said. "I called it my Belker outfit. Remember the detective on *Hill Street Blues*, the one who was always undercover and dressed like a bum? That was the look." He smiled at the memory.

He was assigned to work undercover when he came on duty on July 10, he said. He changed into the Belker, wrapped a walkie-talkie in a paper bag to look like a bottle, and headed over to the campus. He got to the quad near Eldred at 4:15.

"I figured I'd be there for hours and come up empty, but I was there less than forty-five minutes when he came strolling by," he said, laughing. "Right past me. I couldn't believe it. That thing about criminals always returning to the scene of the crime? That isn't true—they usually don't. But there he was. Dressed in the exact same clothes, even. I almost felt guilty, it was so easy to get him."

★

Tuesday, July 10, 1984.

When they catch him outside the hospital, Donovan knows this is the guy. The messy "DAVE" tattoo on his upper right arm is just as I described. The University Circle cops read him his Miranda rights and search him. In one pocket, they find a screwdriver with a sharpened blade, along with a porn magazine called *Black Cherry*. In the other, they find the gold cross that had swayed over my face as he raped me, a pack of Kools, and some marijuana.

"What are you doing on campus?" one of the cops asks.

"I came over here to jog," DAVE says.

They cuff him and take him to the University Circle police station. Donovan reads him his Miranda rights again and tells him he's been arrested for the rape he committed the day before.

DAVE says, "I wasn't even over there yesterday."

Donovan asks about the marijuana in his pocket.

"I'm dying of bone marrow cancer," DAVE says. "I drink beer and smoke weed for the pain." Then he remembers he shouldn't be talking to the cops, and shuts up. He doesn't ask for a lawyer.

The Cleveland police, who will handle the case from here on out, pick him up and take him downtown to the county jail for booking.

CHAPTER SIX

"Do not blurt it out"

Tuesday, July 10.

The day after the rape, hours before DAVE returned to the campus, the case was officially transferred to the Cleveland Police Department's Fifth District, where it landed on the desks of two detectives working the day shift. Both detectives were men; their female partner had the day off.

The report had no leads: no suspect name, other than a tattooed DAVE; no license plate number; no witnesses but the victim—nothing to help them find the rapist right away. They were busy with several other cases, so they put my case aside.

The detectives didn't go over to the crime scene on the Case campus that day, or the next, one of them later testified in court. They didn't call me or ask me to come in and give a statement. They didn't talk to the University Circle police. They went home at 3:30 p.m., the end of their shift, without touching my case.

That night, the University Circle police made the arrest and informed the lead Cleveland detective. He put off calling me, the victim, until the following morning, he testified in court.

When I read this testimony in 2007, I discovered how insignificant my case was to those detectives. I was not surprised. Anyone paying attention in 2007 was well aware of the failures of the Cleveland Police Department, especially when it came to investigating rape. In later years, thousands of rape kits, containing evidence collected from victims but never sent to the state crime lab for DNA testing, would be found stacked in the evidence room. When they were finally tested, starting in 2011, the results would show that more than two hundred serial rapists roamed the city during the 1990s, attacking women while the police set the cases aside.

What if the University Circle police had treated my case with the same disinterest the Cleveland police showed? What if they had decided, when the case went over to the Cleveland police, that it was not their problem anymore, so why bother with a stakeout?

And what if DAVE, never caught, found out I had gone to the cops and decided to follow through on his promise? What if he came to find me?

★

Wednesday, July 11, 1984.

The phone rings. My husband, who is already screening calls to protect me, answers.

I listen to his side of the conversation, and when I hear him say "officer" I want to grab the phone out of his hands and hear whatever the cop has to say myself. Instead I wait, vibrating, every sense lit up, while he talks and listens. Finally he says, "OK," and "Thanks," and hangs up.

"They got him last night," he says. "They want us to come in to view a lineup. He went back to the campus, looking for another victim."

No, I think. *He was looking for me.* I picture him in jail, pacing the perimeter of the cell, enraged. *The bitch promised she wouldn't go to the cops!* He wishes he had killed me when he could have, when he had the point of his homemade dagger at my throat. He vows again that he will find me, someday.

When we'd come to *The Plain Dealer* the year before, I was already slated to be the theater critic and my husband was assigned to news. The first beat they gave him was cops, so he could learn the city. He's spent several months working out of the grungy *Plain Dealer* office at police headquarters, known as the cop shop. He knows his way around the place. He knows people there, the right people, the people who can do things for you.

This will later prove to be as much a bad thing as a good one.

That day, he drives me to the Fifth District station to meet the two detectives, who look like knockoffs of Dennis Franz in *NYPD Blue*, from the $3 ties and the shirt buttons pulling open over their guts to the way they wince and look away when I give them the details of the rape.

I am one of the 1 in 6 women in Cleveland who will report a rape this year. I am one of the 3,734 people who will report a forcible rape in Ohio in 1984. The Cleveland Police Department will not form a sex-crimes unit and institute procedures to deal with rape victims until the following year.

They want me to view the lineup. We drive downtown to police headquarters, a brick fortress pocked with windows so narrow they look like sniper posts. The elevator smells like cigars, with a faint scent of urine underneath.

We wait outside the room while they bring in men from the county jail for my inspection. When they're in place, the detectives usher me into a small room with a one-way mirror, a row of chairs facing it. The lights behind the glass are off, obscuring the men for now while the lieutenant running the procedure explains that seven men matching my description are standing behind the glass. He will turn on the lights, call each one to step forward, turn to the right, then the left, face forward again, and then step back.

He notices my agitation. "You can see them, but they can't see you," he says. "Don't worry." Then he tells me that even if I see the attacker right away, I can't say anything. I have to wait for each man to come forward. "Do not blurt it out," he says. "Take your time and look at each man carefully."

When he turns on the light, I see DAVE at once. He might as well be standing under a spotlight, or be the only man in the lineup. I know he can't see me, but I feel him staring at me through the glass. He tilts his head back, just a bit, and sneers at me. For a few seconds I think I might throw up, right there in front of all the policemen, but I force the nausea back down as the lieutenant calls the first man to step out.

DAVE, second in line, saunters forward when called. He keeps staring at me, a challenge in his expression. The other six men take their turns, but I don't bother to exam them the way the lieutenant instructed. I do notice that DAVE is the only one with a tattoo on his arm. He's also the only one with any energy. The other men look spent, like they've already used up their youth and are expecting nothing from life anymore. When they have all shown themselves, the detective asks me if I see the man who attacked me.

"Yes, I do," I say. "Number Two."

"How certain are you?"

"A hundred percent," I answer, with a quaver in my voice that must have made him wonder how sure I really was. "That's him."

Outside the lineup room, the detectives tell us that they're still getting information on him, but that his name is David Francis and that he was just released from prison on parole the week before.

We head back to the Fifth District station so they can take my statement. One of the detectives moves a pile of papers from a chair, deposits it on top of another pile on the desk, gestures for me to sit down.

"So tell us what happened," he says, rolling a report form into an electric typewriter. I tell him the same thing I told the cop who took me to the hospital, and the second cop who came to interview me there.

He types with his index fingers, concentrating hard, lifting a hand when he wants me to slow down. When I get to the part where I tried to hold the rapist off by telling him I was having my period, he stops typing.

"Were you?" he whispers, flushing a deep red but keeping his eyes on the keys. His partner, sitting across the desk, pretends he didn't hear any of it.

Act by act, I shepherd the detectives through their deep embarrassment about my rape. The lead detective then takes Polaroids of my neck and my hands, which were cut when I tried to push the dagger away, and asks my husband to hold up the back of my shirt so he can photograph what turn out to be my worst injuries: mottled bruises and red, scraped skin across my entire back.

On Thursday, July 12, three days after the rape, the lead detective goes to Eldred Theater. Though the crime scene was never secured and anyone could have disturbed the evidence, he takes twenty-four photographs and collects samples of the dirty red carpet at the back of the stage. He finds a tag from an item of clothing and a small piece of paper, creased and ripped. On it, someone has scrawled three telephone numbers.

The detective takes the evidence to headquarters, tags it, and enters it into the property book. Then he goes over to the county jail to see David Francis.

Twenty-three years later, when I read through the prosecutor's file, the report he writes will tell me about their conversation.

The detective first reads Francis his Miranda rights, then asks him about the rape.

"I don't know what you're talking about," Francis tells him. "I didn't have nothing to do with no rape."

The detective tells him the victim identified him.

"I can't even have sex," Francis says. "I have bone cancer. I haven't had an erection for six months."

"Can you climax?" the detective asks.

"No. I told you, I can't get hard because of the cancer. The doctors told me I have six months to live. That's why they let me out of prison early."

"What were you doing over on the Case campus?"

"I was jogging."

Francis is still in his street clothes. The detective gives him some jail clothes and takes his black pants, the black nylon shirt, the undershorts, a pair of black socks, and a pair of blue-and-white tennis shoes, which he submits to the department's forensic lab to be tested for carpet fiber.

Two days later, on Saturday, July 14, the detective calls the only local number on the piece of paper he found on the stage. A man answers, and when the detective asks, "Who is this?" he answers, "Ed."

"Is David Francis there?" the cop asked.

"No," Ed answers.

"Do you know David Francis?"

"Call back later," Ed says, and hangs up.

Later on in the day, the detective asks his female partner to call the number, hoping a less threatening voice might get more information.

Earlie B. Giles answers the phone.

"Do you know David Francis?" the partner asks.

"Yeah, I know him," Giles says. "I'm his mother's man."

"What is his mother's name?"

"Matia Rodriques."

"Do you know where David Francis is?" the partner asks.

"We heard he was down at the Justice Center, arrested for a rape or something," Giles says.

CHAPTER SEVEN

"He seized her tongue"

When we get home from police headquarters, I know it's time to tell my mother and sisters. Past time. I have invented reasons not to do it, but the reasons no longer apply. I sit on our bed and pick up the phone. I put it down. I do this over and over, unable to call my mother. I want to protect her from this news. I worry that she won't be able to bear it, hearing what has happened to me, her middle daughter. I worry that she will cry or scream, and that I won't be able to bear that.

"I was raped." Why is it so hard to say these three words? They are simple, declarative. But I can't do it. The words will always burn in my throat.

★

It would have helped to know, back then, that this is how almost all rape victims feel. It would have helped to know that we shared a silence as ancient as the Greek myth of Philomela, who was raped by her brother-in-law Tereus. When it was over, Philomela, a virgin, vowed she would tell everyone what he had done, then changed her mind and begged Tereus to kill her.

As Ovid told the story in *Metamorphosis*:

> But Tereus did not kill her; he seized her tongue
> With pincers, though it cried against the outrage,
> Babbled and made a sound something like "Father,"
> Till the sword cut if off. The mangled root
> Quivered, the severed tongue along the ground
> Lay quivering, making a little murmur,
> Jerking and twitching, the way a serpent does
> Run over by a wheel, and with its dying movement
> Came to its mistress' feet. . . .

I didn't know the myth before I was raped, but I had read Philomela's story without realizing it. It has inspired countless variations. Shakespeare revived it in his bloodiest, most savage play, *Titus Andronicus*, with the gang rape and mutilation of Lavinia. T. S. Eliot devotes a stanza to it in *The Waste Land*. In *The World According to Garp*, John Irving created the Ellen James Society, a group of women who voluntarily cut out their own tongues in solidarity with the eleven-year-old Ellen James, who was raped and then mutilated into silence.

In the myth, Tereus holds Philomela hostage in a house in the forest and tells her sister, Procne—his wife—that she is dead. The myth ends with the muted Philomela figuring out how to break her silence: She weaves her story into a tapestry and sends it by secret messenger to Procne. When Procne sees what her husband has done, she rescues Philomela and then proceeds to lose her mind. She kills their son, cuts him up, cooks him, and serves him to Tereus. When the meal is finished, she tells her husband what—or rather, who—he has just eaten.

With this revelation, Tereus goes mad and tries to kill both Procne and Philomela, but the gods intervene and change them into birds. Procne becomes a swallow and Philomela becomes a nightingale. The sisters fly off together.

★

I find refuge in my sister, too. After deciding I can't call my mother, I call Nancy, the person I followed and adored and copied from the time I could toddle after her, calling, "Wait for me," through our years at the University of Minnesota, which I chose because she was going there. Nancy and our little sister, Claire, are both living in New York, Nancy in Brooklyn and Claire on the Lower East Side.

When Nancy answers the phone, I open with a warning. "I have something bad to tell you," I say.

I don't say, "Are you sitting down?" but even so I feel as though I'm following a script. I'm observing myself again, detached from what I'm doing, speaking with a calm that Nancy will always remember. She waits for me to tell her something has happened to our mother. I say the three words. "I was raped."

Without a pause, Nancy starts crying. "Oh, Jo, oh no. Oh, Jo." She keens. "Oh, Jo, poor Jo."

I don't cry with her. I wait and watch and listen from above.

When she quiets, I tell her how it happened. She breaks in with "Oh, Jo" at different points. The scissors. The blood. I don't go into detail about the rape itself. I don't want to cause her more pain.

"I need for you to do something for me," I say.

"What? You want me to get on a plane and come to Cleveland?"

I do. I realize at that moment that I really, really want Nancy there. But first I want something bigger.

"I need you to tell Mom. I can't do it."

Nancy doesn't understand why I can't, but she says she'll take care of it. I lie down on the bed and wait.

Ten minutes later, the phone rings. My mother is not crying.

"It's OK, Jo, it's OK," she says. "Nancy told me what happened. You don't have to tell me."

On the phone, she is the exact opposite of what I expected. But I should have known. After all, she is the mother who put her hand on my forehead when I had a fever, the mother who brought me dry toast and ginger ale on a tray when I was sick, the mother who let me stay home from school even when I wasn't sick, because she could see I had a reason.

On the phone, she becomes what she was all along. She is my mother, but she is also a nurse. Through the decades, while we kids were growing up, she worked just about every job a nurse could have. When we were really little, and they really needed the money, my dad worked at newspapers during the day and she worked night duty at hospitals as a floor nurse. When we were teenagers, she was a rehab center nurse who came home with tales of boys who had been paralyzed in motorcycle accidents, stories she told not just because she wanted to scare us away from motorcycles, which she did, but because she came home still thinking about those poor boys. She was a junior high school nurse for as long as she could stand dealing with hyperactive thirteen-year-old boys. She was a Head Start nurse for preschoolers, teaching their teenage moms how to be mothers. She was a visiting nurse, an HMO nurse, and finally, after going back to college when we were in high school, a certified nurse practitioner who saw patients on her own and worked alongside doctors, not for them.

She had learned, so deep was it in her bones, how to handle a crisis. She knew how to do what I had just learned: how to detach herself and get on with the job.

Now, on the phone, she's in professional mode. She tells me she's going to make plane reservations for me to come home, as soon as the police will let me go. I can stay there as long as I need her. "Everything will be OK," she keeps saying, as much for herself as for me.

When we hang up, I lie back and fall asleep. My husband lies beside me, not touching. An hour or so later, the phone wakes us up.

My mother.

"What happened to the people you were supposed to meet at the theater?" she asks.

"They left. The building was open, though, so I went in."

"No one locked up?"

"No."

"Sue 'em," she says. "Sue the pants off them."

Her anger flattens me. A lawsuit won't help me deal with this. I want it to just go away, not get bigger and more complicated.

"I can't do that," I say. "It wasn't their fault. I was late. They got tired of waiting for me. It was my fault."

My mom doesn't say anything. I don't say anything. Neither of us knows yet what you should say when rape victims blame themselves: "It was not your fault."

It was not your fault, even if you were drunk, even if you were wearing a low-cut minidress, even if you were out walking alone at night, even if you were on a date with the rapist and kind of liked him but didn't want to have sex with him.

Even if you were late. It was not your fault.

But in my self-lacerating mind, that's true only for all the other victims and survivors, not for me. I was late, I was not paying attention, I was stupid, I walked into the theater. It was my fault.

As the days and weeks pass, my mother keeps urging me to sue the university and the theater group and anyone who was on the premises when they left the building wide open.

"They're responsible for this," she says almost every time we talk. "They need to know they made a big mistake."

She needs a focus for her anger, and since David Francis is in jail, her gaze has landed on the people she thinks abandoned me to him. But when she keeps bringing it up, and I keep saying I don't want to do it, all I can see is that she doesn't know me, her daughter. She doesn't know what I need or want. I become the thirteen-year-old who cried all day one Christmas when my mother gave Nancy the coolest suede jacket ever, the color of a fawn, and gave me a wool suit. It was brown tweed, it had a skirt that went below my knees, and it spoke to me. It said: "Your mom hopes you'll consider a career in secretarial work." A suit for a thirteen-year-old. A suit that told me she didn't know me at all. And now here she is, trying to get me into another.

If not a lawsuit, what do I need? I need a sensory deprivation tank guarded by large men with guns. That alone will give me the two things I yearn for: withdrawal from the world, and safety. But I don't know what my mother or my husband can do for me, any more than they know. And if I did, I wouldn't be able to ask for it anyway.

The truth is, I know a lawsuit will lead to a trial, and a trial will lead to me on the stand, testifying to my own foolish, blind actions while expensive lawyers hired by the university and their insurance companies take aim and fire everything they've got at me.

Not long after this conversation, I go to Minnesota. Nancy goes, too. We shop. We eat. We sit around. I do not contact any of my old friends. I live like a convalescent at a sanitarium, overseen by my mother the nurse. Not long ago, I found a photograph from that week: My mother, my sister, and I are in my mother's backyard. I look vacant and completely spent, like I've recently undergone electroshock therapy. My mother and my sister have their arms around me.

By the time I get back to Cleveland, I'm more exhausted than when I left. I get into bed, curl into a fetal position, and stay there.

Only later does it occur to me that after fleeing my mother and her lawsuit, I try to re-create a place I cannot possibly remember: I want to be back inside my mother's womb.

CHAPTER EIGHT

"It's just the law"

As I went through the prosecutor's files in 2007, I came upon a subpoena, addressed to me, ordering me to an "on-site parole hearing regarding David Francis." The site was within the Cuyahoga County jail.

As I read the subpoena, I felt again the old terror lighting up my nerves. To this day, I don't know why that hearing had been necessary.

Up to that point in my career, I had never reported on crime. I had never been inside a jail or prison. I had never been in a courtroom. I had never spoken to a cop, except through my car window as I handed over my license and registration. I had never met a parole officer.

I had seen this country's justice system only in the abstract, from a safe distance. I thought I knew how it worked from news accounts and the little I learned in high school and college classes. I thought it was just, at least most of the time. This was before President George H. W. Bush's escalation of the War on Drugs in 1989 led to the mass incarceration of black men, before DNA testing that began in 1989 exonerated more than three hundred wrongly convicted prisoners, 70 percent of them minority. Even so, I find my ignorance back then breathtaking.

In the summer and fall of 1984, I saw the system up close, though not entirely from the inside. I saw how the game is rigged against defendants. I saw how so many defendants are poor, and black. I saw how easily mistakes can be made, and how unreliable eyewitness testimony is. I understood how the intricate and often impenetrable network of police, prosecutors, courts, parole officers, even defense lawyers—all of whom work together frequently—makes outsiders not only of the defendants but of the victims, too.

★

Six days after the lineup, David Francis's parole officer calls. He tells me what I already knew: Francis was let out of an Ohio prison on parole on July 2, a week before he raped me.

The parole officer tells me that I have to testify in a parole revocation hearing. He can send someone to my house with a subpoena, he says, but it would be easier and faster if he could just give it to me when I come downtown to the county jail. The hearing is scheduled for July 24 at 1:00 p.m., but he'd like me to get there twenty minutes early.

He goes through his explanation so quickly it takes me a minute to catch on to the main thing he's telling me: It's a parole revocation hearing.

"I don't understand," I say. "He's already locked up, so why do you need to revoke his parole now?" As I ask him this, my anxiety flutters, ready to take wing. "I mean, they're keeping him locked up, right? They aren't getting ready to let him go, are they?"

No, no, the guy says. He explains the need for the hearing, which has something to do with the fact that Francis has only been arrested for this new crime, not convicted. If he were convicted, it would be an automatic parole violation; a mere arrest demands a hearing and a witness statement.

I still don't understand. "Why can't they just wait for the trial and conviction? What's the rush?"

The parole officer tries again, but he might as well be speaking to me in another language. He is, I will realize in 2007, when I try to read the Ohio Revised Code and Ohio Administrative Code to figure it out. The codes and laws appear to have been encrypted by the Enigma machine, impossible to decipher for anyone who has not been to Bletchley Park or law school. The maze of rules keeps turning you in different directions and leading you into dead ends.

As the parole guy and I go another few rounds, I begin to think he agrees with me. He doesn't say so, but he finally sighs and says, "Look. It's just the law."

He winds up the conversation fast, telling me that the hearing will take place in lockup, inside the county jail. Oh, and one more thing: I can't bring my husband with me. That's the law, too. He'll see me on the 24th.

I hang up, stunned. I have to go into the jail and sit in a room with the man who raped me, with only a parole officer between us? I decide I can't. I won't. I have not been served with a subpoena that forces me to appear, I have only been called. What can they do if I don't show up? Let him go? It seems unlikely.

My husband isn't stunned when I tell him. He's furious. He calls the parole officer, who tells him I can bring my lawyer with me. He forgot to mention that to me.

One problem: I don't have a lawyer, and we can't afford to hire one.

The prosecutor can't help me. "My" rape case isn't mine at all—it's the state's, as in *The State of Ohio v. David Francis*. The prosecutor works for the people of Ohio. I am just a witness.

My husband calls the Cleveland Rape Crisis Center to see if they have a staff lawyer. They tell him they don't, but they do have an intern from the Case Western law school who might be able to help.

On the day of the hearing, we meet Justine, the law student, outside the county jail, which is in the same complex as the police department and the Justice Center. We leave my husband in the waiting area and go through the metal detectors and the pat-down. Inside, the parole officer introduces himself and leads us to the jail's common area, where the inmates usually eat. They still do, but now bunks line the walls, too. "They're overbooked," he jokes.

Our entrance relieves the boredom of the dozens of inmates, who now have something to do: stare at Justine and me. The room goes quiet; the air feels charged with a furious energy. I shrink into Justine's side and keep my head down as we walk past the staring men and toward my rapist.

The guards, standing in a cluster near the door, ignore it all and continue their conversation. The parole officer leads us to a small, glass-walled room, where the inmates can still watch us. Which they do, intently.

After we sit at a small table, the parole officer opens a file folder and looks through printed forms. When two guards bring David Francis in, Justine grabs my hand under the table and squeezes it.

Perhaps there is a defense lawyer. Perhaps there is a court reporter transcribing everything. I will not remember these details in the years to come. I remember only that David Francis takes the chair directly opposite me, slouches until he is almost parallel to the floor, rests his cuffed hands on the table, and fixes me with a steady gaze that he will hold for the entire hearing. I avoid eye contact, but I can feel his eyes on me.

The parole officer asks me to tell what happened on the afternoon of July 9, 1984. By now I am visibly shaking. Across the table, Francis makes derisive, clicking sounds while I talk. In my peripheral vision, I see him sit up straight when I mention that he kept losing his erection and that he never climaxed. He makes a sound that draws my eyes to his face. When he's sure I'm watching, he purses his lips into a kiss. Justine tightens her grip on my hand. Beyond the glass, the inmates enjoy the unexpected show.

This is my first official testimony. Giving it, I do not feel I now have the upper hand with David Francis. I do not feel safe. This hearing, this stupid, stupid hearing, breaks me into pieces I'm not sure I can put back together. I'm not sure I can testify anymore.

But I have to. In early August, I testify to the grand jury. David Francis is not present. On August 17, the jury indicts him on eighteen counts of rape, kidnapping, felonious assault, attempted rape, gross sexual imposition, and aggravated robbery, each count with a violence specification. At his arraignment, he pleads not guilty. The judge sets bail at $150,000.

We will go to trial in October. I will testify again.

CHAPTER NINE

"I've talked to Johnny. He knows people."

Rape doesn't hurt just one person. It wounds an entire family.

My rape created a vortex that pulled everyone in over the years. My mother, who never got over it. My sisters. My children, who were yet to be born.

The first person it engulfed, though, was my husband. The rape drove him a little mad, in both meanings of the word.

It took me years to understand it. I didn't that summer, not at all. I needed him to be steady and sane. I wanted him to think only about me—about what I needed, about what I felt, about how to keep me safe.

He tried to do that. When he did, though, I felt smothered by his attention. Then, when he talked about the rape, when he showed how angry and frustrated he felt, I thought, *Stop it. This is MY rape, not yours.*

I was wrong. It belonged to both of us.

★

July, 1984. After the parole hearing—they revoke DAVE's parole—I find out what my husband did while I was at my mom's house in Minnesota. He was arranging to hire a hit man. Or hit *men*, I should say.

He tells me one evening in late July when he gets home from work. I'm lying in bed, as is my habit now. I will spend most of the summer here, in a gauzy stupor, like a Victorian lady who has taken to her bed with a vial of laudanum to treat her hysteria, drop by drop by drop.

Every day I get up and get dressed, telling myself it's time to get over it and go back to work. But an hour later I find myself back in the bed, where I stay, alone in the stillness of the house as morning slides into afternoon.

What do I think about, lying there? I do not think. My body takes over, absolutely alert, tensing and freezing every time I hear a creak or thump from our old house. I am like a hunting dog on point. Ears up. Quivering.

(thump)

What was that? Was that a step on the stairs? Was somebody inside the house?

(creak)

Yes. It was definitely somebody. Can I reach the phone and dial without making a sound? How long does it take the police to respond? Does he have time to kill me before they get here?

My watchdog duties drain me, but I can't sleep. I lie in bed, my nervous system flashing messages of panic like Morse code sent out to the universe.

The universe doesn't answer.

Instead: Stillness. A breeze through the window. I start to relax.

But with the next random thump from the house, I can almost see DAVE at the bottom of the stairs, his makeshift dagger in his hand. Of course I know he's in jail. But years of cop shows and horror movies tell me he'll escape and find me. He said he would find me. It's only a matter of time.

Every day, I wait in that bed for my husband to come save me. When he arrives, I listen to him climb the stairs. He always comes into the room like I'm on my deathbed, tentative and quiet, almost tiptoeing.

"Do you need anything?" he'll ask.

Yes. I need everything. I need my old life back, my old self back, my feeling that the world is a safe and good place.

"No," I answer.

I've waited all day for him to come home, but within minutes I itch for him to leave me alone. His presence requires conversation and focus and attention to his emotions, which I cannot give. I resent having to think about his emotions, I resent his needs, I resent his sympathy. I'm awful, and I know it, and I can't stop it.

Now I follow his back-and-forth march across the bedroom floor, wishing he would stop.

The wobbly ceiling fan rotates above me, stirring the hot air. Outside, two boys from a couple of houses down the block play lawn golf. They laugh as they hit balls up and down the row of front yards. This bothered me when we first moved in; I imagined divots pocking our lawn. I almost asked them to get off our lawn, until I remembered I was only thirty years old, and that refrain from the e. e. cummings poem flashed through my head: "too soon! too soon!"

Now I don't care. Dig holes and plant flags in our yard if you want, boys.

An ice-cream truck rolls slowly by, chirping, "It's a Small World." The smell of lighter fluid and smoke drifts in the window.

My husband is talking, laying out the plan. I try not to look at him. I'm crying, but quietly, hoping he won't see the tears welling up. My throat is on fire with the effort to not cry.

"I've talked to Johnny," he says. "He knows people."

I know who Johnny is—he's a guy my husband got to know as a cops reporter—and I have no doubt that Johnny knows people. I just don't want my husband to know the people Johnny knows.

The plan, as put together by Johnny and my husband, is to pay off a guard, or maybe it's two guards, that Johnny knows at the county jail. These guards will slip ground-up glass into David Francis's food. He will eat it, and sometime later he will die a horrible death, bleeding from the inside out, alone in his cell. He will get what he deserves, my husband tells me.

The plan, as I see it, is that the two jail guards will see how ridiculous this plan is and go straight to the FBI to report Johnny, before anyone reports them.

The FBI will go to Johnny, who will tell them it was all my husband's idea. The FBI will come to our house and lead him away in cuffs.

I will be left alone. Alone, with my husband and my rapist in the same county jail.

Lying there in bed, watching my husband pace, I try to figure out how I'll find a lawyer for my husband, how I'll pay the lawyer, how I'll manage bail, how I'll get through my own trial without him.

"You can't do this," I say. "I don't want you to do this. Please. You'll get caught. We could both be arrested."

It occurs to me that I am pleading with my husband the way I had pleaded with David Francis: *Please don't do this. Please.* And then later: *We'll get caught.*

My husband keeps moving, explaining to me that it's a solid plan, he won't get caught, and with the rapist dead I won't have to be afraid anymore. "He's an asshole," he keeps saying. "No one will miss him."

The phone rings. My husband answers. "Hi, Susie," he says. *My mother. Thank God.*

He tells her I'm doing OK. Then I hear him start in on the hit he and Johnny have planned, going through the scheme step by step with her the same way he did with me. I lie back and grind my teeth in time to the fan's rotation. Maybe he won't listen to me, I decide, but if my mother tells him to stop, he'll listen to her.

He tells her about Johnny, what a good guy he is, and about the jail guards and the ground glass. He tells her I don't like the plan, that I don't want him to follow through. Then he stops talking and listens. "Uh-huh," he says. "Uh-huh."

I wait for him to say, "I guess you're right," or "No, it's not too far along. I can stop it."

I wait for him to hand me the phone. I wait to talk to my mother.

Instead I hear him say, "OK, I'll tell her." He hangs up.

"Tell me what? Why didn't she ask to talk to me? What?"

My husband looks at me and smiles. "She said, 'Tell Joanna I'll pay half.'"

★

Years later, I asked my mother if she remembered offering to help pay for a hit man.

"Of course," she said, as though I'd asked her if she pledged to NPR every year. "I thought it was a great idea."

She was my mother. By then I had children, and I was well acquainted with the maternal primate that slumbers deep in my DNA. I had felt her awaken whenever someone hurt or threatened my children. If I allowed that mother to emerge and act on her instinct, to screech and roar and show her teeth, she would. If she could attack, she would.

But in 1984, childless, I burned with feminist outrage. I felt like I was my husband's feudal property, like I was trapped in some medieval time warp. I was the wife in a revenge movie, the woman who gets raped or killed in the first act, triggering her husband—I always think of Mel Gibson playing him—to launch a rampage that produces buckets of blood and at least some visible human entrails.

Vengeance killing has a long and not-so-glorious history. It turns out that revenge movies may resonate with modern audiences because the impulse to seek revenge lives deep in genetically coded behaviors that reach back to our earliest ancestors. That's according to evolutionary psychology, the discipline that looks to Charles Darwin and his theories to answer questions that also live deep within us: Why do we act the way we do? Were we born with all these impulses of jealousy, love, revenge, and everything else, or did we learn them? What do we all share as human beings? What is the purpose of life?

Evolutionary psychologists—I'm generalizing here, since the discipline itself has evolved since it emerged in the mid-'70s—say we can find the answers to many of the mysteries of human behavior and emotion in what Darwin called adaptation and natural selection.

Robert Wright's *The Moral Animal*, published in 1994, was one of the first books to explain and bring mainstream attention to evolutionary psychology. "Altruism, compassion, empathy, love, conscience, the sense of justice—all of these things, the things that hold society together, the things that allow our species to think so highly of itself, can now confidently be said to have a firm genetic basis," he wrote.

Plenty of scientists disagreed with this application of evolutionary biology to human behavior, arguing that it ignored generations of cultural influences. They challenged the idea that the human mind evolved just as the body did. Fights broke out in academia and its journals.

But outside academic circles, the new ideas struck a chord, particularly the evolutionary explanations of sex and mating behaviors, which seemed to endorse infidelity, at least for men.

These were the headline-making observations of evolutionary behavior science: Men are hardwired to seek sex with as many women as possible, driven by the reproductive impulse to spread their genes widely and propel them to future generations. Women, on the other hand, are hardwired to seek a mate with resources and power who will make a parental investment in their offspring, since her reproductive drive is to make sure her offspring—and genes—survive.

But our male ancestors did not want to waste their resources on offspring that did not carry their genes. They wanted monogamy from their mates. So males evolved to ensure their paternity by jealously guarding their mates from other males.

Steven Pinker, the author and experimental psychologist, tells us that the emotion of vengeance may have been tied to this.

In his book *The Blank Slate*, Pinker cites studies of pre-state societies that show that men wage war for reasons other than arguably reasonable ones, like being short of food or wanting to take land from another tribe. "They often raid other villages to abduct women, to retaliate for past abductions, or to defend their interests in disputes over exchanges of women for marriage," he writes.

Pinker goes on to say that "modern states often find themselves at odds with their citizens' craving for revenge. They prosecute vigilantes. . . ."

Which was my point all along. Despite its troubles over the years with burning rivers and fiscal default and so on, Cleveland was arguably still a modern state. It would prosecute my vigilante husband.

CHAPTER TEN

"I can't yell at the pillow"

As July of 1984 seeps into August, I decide to go back to work. I don't think about what, exactly, I will do once I get there. My job requires me to go into dark theaters, a prospect that fills me with dread. But alone in my house I feel trapped, waiting for DAVE to come for me. I need to escape, and in my fog of fear I transform the newsroom into an underground shelter filled with sympathetic friends and lifesaving provisions. My colleagues will shelter me.

This may well be the most naïve thought I have during this whole time period.

The first day, the walk from the door to my desk feels like a perp walk. I know that everyone knows. It's a newsroom—of course everyone knows. Reporters, tireless gossips that we are, have honed our skills into a professional asset. We regard secrets much the way we regard the free booze at weddings and wakes: We can't stay away from the open bar or the open secret.

No one says anything to me. People avoid walking past my desk, or pretend to be looking somewhere else if they happen to pass me on the way to the cafeteria. I feel alone in a spotlight, observed by an audience who does not want to be there and keeps averting its collective gaze.

I have nothing to do. Nothing. My editor, all hard-boiled bluster, comes straight out of the era of *The Front Page*, when reporters wore hats and chased scoops and their editors fumed. He gets his gray hair buzzed every couple of weeks and wears a wide tie with short-sleeved dress shirts, and, since they will not ban smoking in the newsroom until the following year, he lights up a cheap cigar every afternoon. I consider this a hostile act against a staff he makes no secret of disliking.

In my absence, he has assigned all my reviews and stories to other people, and when I return he doesn't bother to give me anything else. He can barely look at me. I sit at my desk and try to look busy. I try not to cry. After a couple of hours, I tell my editor I have to go home. He nods but doesn't look at me.

I go back the next day, and the next. Now I feel like I'm carrying an exotic disease and have been quarantined without anyone having informed me. No one says anything. I know they're embarrassed; I know they have no idea what to say to me. In any case, they've probably picked up a signal I don't even know I'm giving off, a signal that says, "Please don't talk about it." They're right. The prospect of receiving a simple "I'm sorry" unnerves me, because I know I will have no control over my reaction. I've experienced this before: When my father had a heart attack on a tennis court and died when I was twenty-two, it was such a shocking and unexpected event,

I could not bear for anyone to offer sympathy. If they did, I would mutely nod and turn away, tears pooling in my eyes.

I can't allow myself to cry at work. We're in the old, open newsroom, cubicles still in the distant future, with desks pushed against desks, phones ringing, people talking. The place still has the pneumatic tubes that once carried copy upstairs to the typesetters. It would serve nicely as the set for a revival of *The Front Page*, if it weren't for the massive computer terminals that have landed on the desks like spaceships from a 1950s sci-fi movie, one computer for every two reporters.

It is also, still, a very male atmosphere. A couple of years later, I will share a computer with the TV critic, a woman whose breasts are as big as mine—a cross I have borne from seventh grade on. One day, a reporter will saunter over and say, "What is this, the pulchritude corner?" Smiling. Waiting for one of us to answer.

The band of brothers gets away with this stuff. They also get away with leaving in the middle of the day to go to "lunch" at the Headliner, the joint on the next block where the smoke forms thick clouds over a wooden bar, the bar stools have cracked vinyl seats indented with the butts of generations of reporters, and the bartenders will run a tab if they know you. More than once an editor has had to send a copy aide over to the Headliner to haul a reporter back to the newsroom for an assignment.

So there I am, in the middle of the old newsroom, trying to look busy. You've heard the Tom Hanks line, "There's no crying in baseball"? Well, there's really, really no crying in newsrooms. I can no more cry in that open newsroom than

Carl Bernstein could have cried on Bob Woodward's shoulder in the middle of the *Washington Post* newsroom.

Then, a few days in, two colleagues approach me.

The first is a reporter I've talked to a couple of times. We're just starting to be friends. She asks if I want to go for a walk. We go outside, into the glorious summer afternoon, and she keeps her eyes on her feet hitting the sidewalk as she tells me about the time she was in high school and went for a hike in the ravine near her school. It was the middle of the day. There were three boys, older than her. Two held her down while the third raped her. Then they traded places. She didn't know them. She never reported it and never told anyone; she was afraid her immigrant parents would freak out, not let her out of their sight, and even, possibly, not let her go away to college. She never again went for hikes alone, and she had never talked about it until now, with me.

The other is a colleague I don't know at all. An editor asks her to talk with me, and so I find myself in the cafeteria, sitting across from a woman so tough I will always imagine her wearing military fatigues. You can bet no one in the newsroom comments on her pulchritude. I can tell she doesn't want to be here, talking about her own rape. Her jaw tenses with every word. She tells me it happened in the parking lot of the newspaper, at night. A stranger slashed her tires and waited for her to get to her car, then approached her to offer help. She doesn't go into detail. She did report it, the police came, but they never caught him.

Both women tell me what happened to them as though they're reporting it to the police—just the facts, no emotion, exactly the way I told the people who needed to be told. They don't talk about the things I need to hear and they need to say: how scared they are now, how they wake up in the middle of the night sometimes with their hearts pounding, how hard it is to be alone, how they never go outside at night, how they battle this feeling of shame but still feel it to their core.

None of us talk about it with each other again.

And I'm OK with that—more than OK. I don't want to talk about my rape or anyone else's.

Therapists, though, consider it their job to get you to talk about it—"it" being whatever you're trying not to talk about.

My husband and I go to the first therapist, in what will be a long line of therapists, shortly after I go back to work. She has filled her office with floor cushions and pillows, but no furniture. We lean into the cushions while she sits on top of one, like a Yogi. The first thing she tells us is that most marriages don't survive this kind of trauma. She gives us a statistic, a pretty alarming one, though I won't remember it later; maybe 80 percent? I barely listen to her warning. I'm sure it won't happen to us. We separated once, in Minneapolis, but we got back together stronger than ever. The therapist's statistics must be for marriages that are already in trouble. I don't realize that I'm indulging myself in more magical thinking of the "It won't happen to me" school. I should have learned from the rape: Nothing happens until it happens to you.

Next, the therapist has us both tell our stories of the rape. I tell mine the usual way—just the facts, ma'am—though by now I'm leaving out some of the details, the ones that made the cops wince and look away. My husband tells her about the hospital, the police station, the lineup, and the parole hearing. He cries as he tells it.

Neither of us mentions the one thing that we most need to talk about to save our marriage: the hit-man plan. Which is dead, as far as I know. After several more crying fits, I've finally persuaded my husband to stop the plan, though I have this nagging doubt that keeps surfacing. Maybe one day a cop will call and tell me David Francis died in jail. Or maybe Johnny or one of the jail guards called the whole thing off, and my husband found someone else. I have no idea how far he went with it.

The hit-man plan, dead or not, marked the moment when I felt I couldn't trust my husband to be rational. His plan, and my bitterness about having to deal with it when I was most vulnerable, opened a fault line in our marriage.

On our second appointment, the therapist asks me if I feel angry. In fact, yes, I feel plenty of anger—toward my husband, however, not the rapist. But I can't talk about the plan. It embarrasses me, deeply, and I'm not sure if she would have to report my husband to some authority.

"No, I'm not angry," I say.

She feels that I need to allow myself to be angry. She gives me one of the many pillows in her office and tells me to pretend it's the rapist.

"Punch him," she says. "Yell at him. Tell him what he did to you. Let it out."

I give the pillow a halfhearted punch.

"Now go ahead and yell," she says.

I stare at the pillow. After some thought, I decide I have nothing to say to the pillow.

"I can't yell at the pillow," I say. "I'm not sure I'm feeling anger right now."

★

I believed that for the longest time. Twenty-three years later, when I decided to look for David Francis, it occurred to me that the therapist was right: My anger was there, waiting to attack, but I was afraid of it. It was too large, too unruly, too honest. There was no way I, raised to be a polite girl, could roar my terrible roar, and gnash my terrible teeth, and show my terrible claws.

So I banished my anger to a faraway cave, and in its absence I felt . . . nothing. Emptiness. I was a ghost, my body made of vapor. Maybe it couldn't feel anything.

I welcomed this absence of feeling. I decided that it meant I'd recovered. In my inner dialogues, I talked to myself like the nastiest right-wing curmudgeon on talk radio, telling myself, "Get over it! You survived. Now stop thinking about it, stop acting like a victim, and for God's sake stop whining. Just get on with your life."

So I did. After three sessions, we quit seeing that therapist.

And after the trial, we stopped talking about the rape. We both thought about it—a lot, as it turned out—but we did not mention it.

CHAPTER ELEVEN
The question

But before the endless silence, we had to get through the trial. And before the trial we had to work with the prosecutor. The prosecutor whose files and notes I had on my desk in 2007.

Allan Levenberg ranked as the top lawyer in the county prosecutor's major trials division, which handles homicide and rape cases. He was a compact man, so fond of order and precision that the other prosecutors called him "The Brownshirt" behind his back. Unlike a lot of lawyers I met later as a reporter, whose offices resembled landfills of paper and file boxes, he kept his as neat as an army barracks before inspection.

Two decades after he worked on my case, when I began digging into it as a reporter, I discovered that he had, in fact, been in the military. He was an officer and a Green Beret, and volunteered for two combat tours in Vietnam. He led paratroopers in jumps and learned to speak Vietnamese. The year after my trial, he joined the federal Organized Crime Strike Force, which was busy dismantling the last remaining vestiges of the Cleveland Mafia, thanks to the testimony of its former boss, Angelo "Big Ange" Lonardo, the highest-placed mafioso ever to turn snitch, and a favorite witness of then U.S. attorney Rudy Giuliani.

Levenberg died in 1998 of leukemia. I found his obituary in the *Plain Dealer* library. His final cases, it said, dealt with an FBI sting that went after corrupt Cuyahoga County jail guards.

★

In late July of 1984, before I'm supposed to appear in front of the grand jury, my husband and I go to meet Levenberg in the Cuyahoga County Justice Center, a monolithic, twenty-six-story tower near Lake Erie that was built in the mid-'70s in the heavy, fortresslike style of architecture known as Brutalist. Which is a fine description for what went on in there.

The entrance, a three-story concrete-and-brick space, is meant to be a light-filled atrium. It feels more like a Stalinist's idea of a mall food court. Few people linger there after getting their morning coffee. The elevators are slow and always crowded, especially in the mornings when lawyers and witnesses are trying to get to the courtrooms on the upper floors. The prosecutor's office has a sad little lobby with exhausted furniture and a clerk who sits behind a sliding glass window, guarding a hive of tiny assistant prosecutors' offices.

We meet with Levenberg in one of those tiny offices, squeezing ourselves into the two chairs wedged between his desk and the wall.

Levenberg will prove to be stern and flinty in his dealings with me, but that day he's almost gleeful as he talks about my case, which, he makes clear, is not really my case. He represents the people of the State of Ohio, he tells us. I am just the main witness.

★

I now know why Levenberg was so jolly that day. Prosecutors know how difficult it is to bring a rape case to a jury, even now, particularly in cases where the victim knows the perpetrator: date rapes, acquaintance rapes on college campuses, rapes by family members and friends. If the alleged rapist claims the sex was consensual, the jury has to weigh the victim's word against the defendant's.

In 1984, legislators and courts had begun to change rape laws, which until then had, among other things, held that a husband could not be accused of raping his wife, allowed defense lawyers to present the victim's sexual history as evidence, and required a corroborating witness to the rape.

These had their roots in the earliest known written laws. Susan Brownmiller's indispensable 1975 best-seller, *Against Our Will: Men, Women and Rape*, taught many readers—including me—the history of rape and the laws governing it. I first read it in a women's studies class, a class where I discovered how much I did not know about the hard-fought crusade women had waged, and were still waging, for the independence and rights I took for granted. At the time, I didn't fully appreciate how revolutionary some of Brownmiller's ideas were.

I am indebted to Brownmiller for her history, which started with the Babylonian Code of Hammurabi dating to 1780 B.C.

Back then, what happened to me would not have been a rape at all, simply because I was married. Under the Babylonian Code, only virgins could be raped. Married women who were unfortunate enough to be raped were instead considered adulterers, and if their husbands did not absolve them of this "crime," they were bound and thrown into the river along with their rapist. Later versions of rape laws—in the Old Testament, for instance—called for stoning to death both the rapist and his victim.

In the Code of Hammurabi and later, raped virgins were exempt from these suspicions, though the laws still did not consider them to be the victims of a crime. The victims were instead their fathers, since women were legally the property of their fathers until they married. Therefore, rape was a property crime, the theft of a woman's valuable, marriage-ready virginity.

Through subsequent centuries, rape remained an offense against the woman's father or husband, usually resolved with a payment to the father and, sometimes, the daughter's forced marriage to her rapist, since no other man would want a defiled virgin as a wife.

In English law—which served as the template for much of American law—rape was not defined as a forced sexual crime until the twelfth century, though even then the victim was the father or husband, because he had lost the honor and value of the woman.

These ancient laws also reflected a widespread suspicion that women accusing men of rape were lying—a belief system that is still operative today. Almost every time a star athlete or celebrity is accused of rape, for example, there's an inference that the charge is false, brought by a scorned, or vindictive, or drunk, or willing woman against an innocent man. We see it in the Bible, in the story of Joseph the slave and the wife of his master, Potiphar. This wife lusted after Joseph, who refused to lie with her. Scorned by a slave, the story goes, she got even by accusing him of rape. It shows up centuries later in British law, in the cautionary words of a judge during the seventeenth century. Rape, said Lord Matthew Hale, is "an accusation easily to be made and hard to be proved and harder to be defended by the party accused, tho never so innocent."

In America, rape was entangled with slavery and, later, the Jim Crow laws. Before the Civil War, masters were free to rape the women they kept as slaves—though no one called it rape—and could even purchase them for that single purpose. These attitudes remained long after emancipation, when rape was, in much of America, legally considered a crime only if a black man raped a white woman. As for black women, neither the law nor the general culture protected them from rape, while white men accused of rape enjoyed the fullest protection of both.

During the 1800s, white men who raped white women were fairly safe from the law, since women needed to prove both their own chastity and their physical resistance to bring an accusation against a white man. Police and juries wanted to see violent injuries on the victim's body, or at least torn and bloodstained garments.

If the alleged rapist was black, he faced a jury of white men and punishments of hanging or castration.

This was just a little of the history behind one of the first things Levenberg said to me that day we went to meet him in July of 1984.

★

"You're the ideal witness."

If Levenberg were a man who found anything in the world delightful or humorous, he would laugh, he is so happy. As it is, he smiles a tight smile and continues.

He explains that I'm the perfect witness because I'm a journalist, trained to observe details and remember them. But I know what he really means. To him, I'm the perfect victim because I happen to fulfill just about all the requirements of a woman accusing a man of rape, going back to before the Civil War. I am white, educated, and middle-class. I resisted, and I have a cut on my neck, bruises still healing on my spine, and a torn and blood-stained blouse to prove it. I immediately ran to report the rape.

Needless to say, David Francis is the perfect defendant: black, poor, and uneducated, with a criminal record.

If only I'd been a virgin, too, Levenberg would have had everything he needed for a swift and successful trial.

He tells my husband and me that, as ideal as I am as a witness, he does not have to rely on me alone. They have the scrap of paper the detectives found on the stage at Eldred, the one with the phone number for David Francis's mother.

Levenberg says he will prepare me for the trial later, closer to the court date. He tells me not to worry. "This is a strong rape case," he says. "This is a very strong rape case."

I try to stop, but the closer we come to the trial date, the more I worry. What if the jury notices the inconsistencies in my descriptions? In one statement, I said Francis had very dark skin; in another statement, just dark skin. Or maybe medium. Did I say "light" at one point? I can't remember. And if I had been face-to-face with him for an hour, why couldn't I answer the cop when he asked if he had wispy facial hair or sideburns? Why didn't I see the tattoo until we were outside? Why couldn't I say exactly how tall he was? Just how observant was I, really?

Summer ends, fall begins. I continue to collect worries, pinning them to my brain like rare butterflies.

Levenberg calls from time to time to report developments. In September, Francis's public defenders ask for a pretrial hearing to submit motions. The court schedules it for September 13, but Levenberg says I don't need to be there. That morning, in any case, it's canceled. Levenberg calls to tell me that the night before, the jail guards found a knifelike weapon in Francis's cell. The court reschedules the hearing for the day before the trial. In October, I get a subpoena to appear in the courtroom of Judge Harry Hanna at 9:00 a.m. on Monday, October 22.

A few days before that, my mother flies to Cleveland to help me get through it. I'm still upset by her pressure to sue the university and her enthusiasm for my husband's plot to hire a hit man, but I need her. At this point, my anxieties are ringing bells and setting off fireworks.

Levenberg calls my husband and me in to prepare me for my testimony. He takes me through the questions he'll ask me, and tells me how the defense lawyers will probably question me. He says they will focus on my ability to describe and then identify the rapist when I was so terrified, and to see details in a dark theater. He talks about them like they're our enemy and we're about to go into battle.

The defense lawyers are right about the eyewitness identification, I will learn in the coming years when I cover a few trials. After DNA evidence becomes available and affordable in the 1990s, lawyers for the Innocence Project and others start using it to help inmates who have credible claims of innocence. Of the 312 DNA exonerations from the first one in 1989 to 2013, mistaken eyewitness testimony was to blame in 73 percent of the wrongful convictions. These eyewitnesses probably told juries that they were 100 percent certain of their identifications.

In 1984, we don't have DNA, but we have something just as good, if not better. We have the tattoo.

Levenberg loves the tattoo. "How nice he gave us his name," he says. "It's like a rapist's business card."

After about an hour of talking about the case, Levenberg asks my husband to leave the room—he has something he wants to ask me alone.

When we're alone, Levenberg leans back in his chair and regards me across his desk.

"So I need to know one last thing," he finally says.

Another pause.

"Why the *hell* did you go into that theater?"

CHAPTER TWELVE
The answer

I will forever remember Levenberg asking me that question, but I will not remember my answer. Whatever I said, I know it was not what I wanted to tell him, which was a simple, declarative "Fuck you."

After not saying "Fuck you," I left his office, collected my husband in the waiting area, went down in the elevator, walked to the car, drove home, and went inside. Then, and only then, did I allow myself to cry. Which I proceeded to do for about five hours, while my mother sat with me and occasionally rubbed my back or hugged me or said, "Oh, sweetie," and my husband paced and worked up a fury at this new enemy, Levenberg, who sent him out of the room so he could make me feel like the whole thing was my fault. I could see his mind working. I knew he was thinking about revenge.

"Well, it *was* my fault," I said, with great huffing and stammering between my sobs. "I did go into that theater."

Why? Why was I so stupid? My own prosecutor, the one who told me I was an ideal witness, had just shown his hand. He thinks I'm an idiot, not ideal in any way.

★

I hated and distrusted Levenberg from then on, even when I had to depend on him during the trial. At the same time I knew, but could never admit, that his question was reasonable. Not long ago, a lawyer I know told me Levenberg probably asked it because he thought the defense lawyer would ask on his cross-examination of me, and he wanted me to be ready. But if that was the case, why would he send my husband out of the room? I suspect Levenberg thought the question would anger him.

It turned out that the defense lawyer never did ask me why I went into that theater. But when I decided to write about the rape, more than two decades later, Levenberg's question remained unanswered.

Remember that warning that went off in my head, when the stranger in the hallway asked me if I wanted to see the lighting? Twenty-three years later, I can recall every breath of that moment: his casual offer, the smell of the Kool he was smoking, the instant of alarm I felt, my all-too-brief hesitation before I went ahead. In that moment I knew I shouldn't have anything to do with this stranger.

I went into the theater for one reason: Because he was a young black man.

I could not allow myself to be the white woman who fears black men.

My decision came out of what James Baldwin called "that panic-stricken vacuum in which black and white, for the most part, meet in this country."

Would I have gone into the theater if a white man with claims of working on the lighting had suggested it? I don't have an answer to that question, no matter how many times I ask it of myself. I do know that I was far more likely to be attacked by a white man. Interracial rapes, despite the media depictions and the drummed-up cultural panic that goes back to the Reconstruction era, are much rarer than same-race rapes. According to the Bureau of Justice Statistics, white victims are raped by white assailants in 74.9 percent of reported sexual assaults. Only 16.4 percent of the cases involve black offenders and white victims. When the victim is black, the offender is also black in 74.8 percent of the cases.

This comparatively low incidence of interracial rape may exist, in part, because rapes by family members and acquaintances are far more common than rapes by strangers. The BJS statistics show that only 25 percent of rapes are committed by strangers, versus 69.9 percent by nonstrangers.

But here's the most startling statistic in the BJS report: When the victim is black, the reported offender is white in 0 percent of the cases. Instead, the reported offender's race is "Not known or not available" in 25.2 percent of the cases.

How can this be true? Statistics of reported rapes do not tell the entire story, rape crisis experts say, because many rapes go unreported. The reasons are many, but given the grave distrust of the police in much of the black community, it's not hard to imagine that black victims would not choose to call them—particularly to report a rape by a white man.

★

When I left my body and watched my rape, the primitive fear center of my brain was busy recording everything and storing it up for future panic, a panic that embedded itself and still dictates my reaction when I am alone somewhere with a man I don't know. My heart gallops without warning. My breathing grows shallow. I flush. My startle reflex, when anyone approaches me from behind, is so exaggerated I unnerve people, who find themselves apologizing to me without quite knowing what they did wrong.

My body still screams "Danger!" when I'm alone and a strange man approaches, black or white. But because of David Francis, for many years the fear was sharper with black men. I started going through red lights when I drove through Hough late at night. I averted my gaze on sidewalks when a young black man came toward me. I stepped out of elevators when I found myself alone in one with a black man, and walked up the stairs instead.

The first time that particular fear revealed itself I was in New York on assignment. I had arranged to rent an apartment near Lincoln Center because, I told my editor, it was cheaper than a hotel and I could make my own breakfast. But in truth

I yearned to be someone else for two weeks, a young single woman in New York, embarking on a brilliant career. Safe in the crowds of the city, I wanted to walk everywhere, fearless and anonymous.

On the second or third day, I was alone in the building's elevator when it stopped at a high floor. A black man in a leather coat got on. I nodded at him, he nodded at me: the usual elevator good manners. But even as I nodded, a panic attack ambushed me. I slumped against the back wall of the elevator, dizzy and sick, and steadied myself by focusing on the lit-up floor numbers that marked our slow descent. I was behind the man, but the elevator was lined with mirrors. I prayed he wouldn't notice me. I prayed I would not throw up. When the doors opened, he exited without a glance back.

The rest of the time I was there, I walked up and down the twenty-eight flights of stairs to the apartment.

The fears, the panic attacks, the thrumming heart—this new fear of black men shamed me more than the rape.

When Chris Rock said, "I was born a suspect. I can walk down any street in America and women will clutch their purses tighter, hold on to their Mace, lock their car doors," he was talking about me. I hated that he was talking about me.

It didn't matter that I worked with black men, that I had black neighbors and friends. I could hear the arch response echo in my head: "Oh, you have a black friend?"

I remembered, from my Bible as Literature class in college, what St. Paul said to the Romans: "I have the desire to do what is good, but I cannot carry it out. For I do not do the good I want to do, but the evil I do not want to do." My fear was evil, and it was stronger than my will.

I wanted, desperately, to uphold my values and judge others on the content of their character. But how can one judge the character of a man waiting in a theater lobby in an otherwise empty building, smoking a Kool?

CHAPTER THIRTEEN
"It's better than TV"

October 1984.

As the trial gets closer, my brain shifts to obsessing over more familiar territory: What to Wear. I've seen courtrooms in action only in movies and on TV shows, a predicament that has transformed the witness box into a stage. I have been cast in the role of the victim, but I have no idea to how dress the part, let alone play it. For several nights, I have the Freudian dream that I am naked among the clothed, desperate to cover myself while wondering why I am naked.

Intrinsically tied to the "What to Wear" question is the much bigger question that has ruled my life since I was ten years old and my uncle called me the chubby sister, to distinguish me from Nancy, "the smart sister," and Claire, "the pretty sister."

I am, and forever will be, the daughter of a mother who never stopped trying to lose those "last" five pounds, who said the last-five-pounds thing so often I believed her. Now I look at pictures of her from my childhood, from our years in Miami, and I see that she was as slender and glamorous as Jackie Kennedy. I remember how beautiful she was, in her chic, spaghetti-strap dresses, the Bernardo sandals that made her tanned legs look long and elegant, the slim white slacks she wore with sleeveless blouses that tied at the waist. Every night, she put her hair in pin curls, with X-crossed bobby pins, a ritual that somehow produced a Jackie bouffant in the morning. She wore Tabu perfume, a dark, musky scent that instantly takes me back to evenings when my sisters and I would sit on her bed and watch her dress to go out to parties. She smoked like Jackie Kennedy, too, mostly to keep her weight down. She took us to Virginia every summer to visit our cousins, and on the long car trips we vied for the seat in front, right next to her, where she would hand us her pack of Kents and ask us to light a cigarette for her. I loved putting the cigarette between my lips and working that glowing little push-in lighter in the dashboard.

In one photo, my mother is in a hospital cafeteria, her starched white nurse's cap pinned to her hair, a cup of coffee on the table and a cigarette in her hand. Years later, she told me that when she was in nurses' training, hospitals kept open jars of amphetamines in the drug dispensary for student nurses and residents who were pulling twenty-four-hour shifts. "It was like a candy jar," she said, delighted by the memory. "We'd just dip in whenever we wanted."

Still, she dieted. "I just want to break 130," she said over and over, which meant she weighed 131 or 132 and really wanted to starve herself down to 125. But like every women's magazine that has ever existed, she promoted dieting one moment and featured fattening food the next. Her cooking repertoire consisted of boiled hot dogs served with baked beans, hamburgers and tater tots, London broil and baked potatoes. For many years, every Sunday she made a meal from her Georgia farm childhood: real fried chicken, corn on the cob, mashed potatoes, and string beans that she had cooked for hours with a big chunk of salt pork, until the surface of the water reflected light like an oil spill. While we ate, she smoked.

When I was fourteen, she took me to a Weight Watchers meeting in a basement room of the public library. Her effort to be helpful felt only like criticism. I sulked in the back row, behind the women in velour tracksuits, listening to the energetic leader tell us how to cook Weight Watchers meals that our husbands and children would eat. I am not sure whom I hated more at that moment, my mother or myself.

The first time I remember my mother telling me I looked thin, her ultimate compliment, was when she saw me after the two-month bout of dysentery that had started in Bolivia, on a trip my husband and I took through South America when we were twenty-three. "You're so thin!" she said, before she even hugged me. It makes me sad now to remember how happy that made me feel. We joked that we should bottle the Bolivian water and sell it to Americans as the latest diet craze. We would call it: La Paz.

★

So. This is the body that I still scorn, the body that disappoints me, the body that David Francis cut and violated, the body

I still scrutinize every morning in the mirror, focusing on its imperfections.

I want to think of it as the strong body that survived, but my mind fails me.

As the trial draws near, the worries about how I will look to the jury help me avoid thinking about the rape and what I will have to tell the jury. My mother takes me to the mall to buy some new clothes. After all that worry, I will have no memory of what I end up wearing.

My trial is far less dramatic than movies had led me to believe it would be. I will learn this from reading the 499-page court reporter's transcript many years later, not from being there to watch it unfold, because I am not allowed in the courtroom except to testify. It's common practice to sequester witnesses, and so I wait outside Courtroom 17C, in an open area shared with three other courtrooms.

As rolling schedules of pretrials and hearings come and go in the other courtrooms, the waiting area fills up with victims waiting to testify and families there to support the accused, almost all of them black. The days I spend in that waiting area I see, for the first time, an American reality I knew only in the abstract: In Cuyahoga County, as in the rest of America, the criminal courts are filled with people who are black or poor, victims and defendants alike. Often, I was the only white person in the waiting area.

Census statistics show that African-Americans make up 13.6 percent of the U.S. population, a percentage mirrored almost exactly in Cuyahoga County. But in the latest Bureau of Justice Statistics, from 2013, 37 percent of imprisoned men were black while 32 percent were white.

In 2013, the Sentencing Project, an advocacy and research group, reported to the United Nations that African-American males are six times more likely to be incarcerated than white males, and warned: "If current trends continue, one of every three black American males born today can expect to go to prison in his lifetime ... compared to one of every seventeen white males."

*

The trial begins on Monday, October 22, 1984, with jury selection. It takes about two hours. The judge then sends the jurors and alternates, the lawyers and the bailiff on a bus out to Eldred Theater for a jury view requested by the defense lawyers, who hope to show how dark the theater is, how hard it would be to see anything or anyone clearly.

We return to court on Tuesday, October 23, at 1:00 p.m. My husband and my mother leave me in the waiting area to go watch the trial, but they promise to come out during breaks to update me.

"Levenberg was great," my husband reports after the opening statement, smiling as though Levenberg is now some hero who'd ridden in to save the day. The smile feels like a betrayal. We're supposed to hate Levenberg, together. I still hate him. I need him, too: I need him to win this and save me. I hate needing him. I gulp these feelings down and smile back, nodding. My husband bends to hug me before rushing back to the courtroom for the defense's opening.

I shift on the straight-backed chair, trying and failing to get comfortable. Time passes. People come and go from the other courtrooms, but the door to 17C remains closed, a silent rebuke to my mistakes and failures.

I keep my eyes on that door and wait, a supplicant to a powerful secret society. Inside, they are talking about me. They are calling me "Miss Connors." They are going over what I did that day, and what was done to me.

The waiting area empties. Close to the end of the day, a sheriff's deputy emerges from the courtroom and walks toward me, his belt sagging under the weight of his hardware.

"You've been called," he says.

My heart is a wild bird when I enter the courtroom. I search for my husband and mother and find them in the first row, turned toward me with expressions they intend to be reassuring. I fix my eyes on them, trying to obliterate the rest of the courtroom, but I can feel David Francis watching me go down the aisle.

The room is still and silent. I walk through a fog to the judge's bench.

No one has come to watch the trial, with the exception of an older couple I don't recognize. They turn out to be court groupies who come to the Justice Center to watch trials almost every day. "It gets us out of the house, and it's better than TV," the woman tells my mother one day.

After the oath I take my place on the witness stand, which puts Francis directly in front of me, slouching at the defense table between his two lawyers. He sits up straight and studies me; a hard challenge is his gaze, his final attempt at intimidation. I look away, toward the jurors, but my eyes slip back to him to see if he's still watching me. He is. I see that he's made himself presentable with a white knit polo shirt, his hair arranged in neat cornrows.

"He's getting ready to be pretty for the big guys in prison," my husband says later, trying to cheer me up. He doesn't. His sarcasm infuriates me. I push my anger down and pretend it isn't there.

Over the coming years, I will see enough trials as a reporter to know that they are slow and tedious. Even murder trials can make you feel as though you're stuck in an SAT exam that will never end, especially when the coroners take the stand. Prosecutors have to provide evidence for each count of the indictment, and at the same time counter any doubts the defense might try to introduce during their part of the trial. Since Francis is charged with eighteen counts, Levenberg has to go through them one by one, building a numbing and disjointed story that begins with questions like, "How long have you worked at *The Plain Dealer*?" and "Where did you park when you got out to Case Western Reserve University?" and "What kind of vehicle?"

He spends seven pages of transcript asking me about the lighting in the theater and how well I could see that day. At one point, he asks me to take off my glasses and tell him how many fingers he's holding up.

I answer these like a star expert hired for the trial, but then Levenberg comes to the point of what happened in the theater.

I can feel my face flush red when he asks: "You say there came a point in time when as a result of the conversation that you were having with this individual about the lights, you became aware in your own mind that there was something untoward, that something didn't jive here, is that right?"

"Yes."

"What, if anything, did you do at that time?"

My voice starts to tremble. As I go through the story once again, I float from the witness box and enter that other dimension. I can see myself on the stage. I hear myself say, "I think I'll wait outside." I feel him grab me from behind. "No," I say. I feel the metal at my throat.

Levenberg asks: "What happened at that time?"

From afar, I answer.

"I saw my hand and it had blood on it and I became terribly frightened and I thought I was going to be killed."

My voice breaks on the word "killed." I stop talking, trying to hold back the flood of my fear and my grief and my shame. I tell myself I cannot cry in court.

When I lose that battle, the judge leans over with a box of tissues, looking at me with the face of a concerned father. That makes me cry even more.

Levenberg waits while I dry my tears and clear my throat, trying to get rid of the tightness. He goes on, easing me back with softball questions like, "This all took place there on the stage, is that correct?"

After a few of those, he asks, "What was the next thing that occurred?" and I have to resume the story.

"I was saying, 'Oh, please, don't do anything to me,' " I say. "I thought I was going to be murdered." The tears come again, but this time I am not watching myself from above. I am in my body, fully in it, and I am telling the people in the courtroom what I felt that day.

I was going to be murdered. I would die on that stage.

Now I can't stop the tears with tissue.

"Your Honor, I think this might be an appropriate time to stop," Levenberg says. The judge calls a recess until the next morning.

I go home with my husband and my mother, who hover over me with the gentleness of hospice volunteers. I don't sleep. At 9:15 on Wednesday, October 24, we begin again. Levenberg leads me through each count of the rape, each separate sexual act. It takes over two hours, longer than the rape itself.

Then the defense starts the cross-examination. The two public defenders, stuck with a defendant who has tattooed his own name on his arm, will try to build a case of mistaken identity. They failed with their first attempt, a motion to get the lineup thrown out on the grounds that David Francis was the only one in it with a "DAVE" tattoo.

The lead defense lawyer, John Adams, asks in as many ways as he can about how dark it must have been in the theater, suggesting that it was too dark, really, to see much. He goes over how terrified I was, too terrified to make a real identification. He asks if I looked more at the weapon than at the rapist. He shows me photos of the men in the lineup. Don't I agree that most of them do not fit my description?

When it is over at last, I have to leave the courtroom again, still sequestered in case I am called back to the stand. Again I wait, alone, for my mother and husband to tell me what's happening. After the ER doctor testifies, my mother rushes out with exciting news.

"The doctor described you as thin! A thin woman!"

Another time, my husband comes out to report on the defense's first alibi witness. She's twenty-one, he says, she has a one-year-old child, and she describes David Francis as a friend. She is the one from the jail records, who visited him in jail several times. In the trial transcript, one of the first questions the defense lawyer asks her is, "Where do you presently reside?"

She responds, "What that mean?"

Once they establish her address, she testifies that the last time she saw David Francis was on July 9, at around four in the afternoon. They were at her apartment with her old man, her mother, and a couple more friends. "We just be sitting around talking, looking at TV, that's all," she says.

The lawyer moves the story along, asking, "Did there come a time when Mr. Francis left your home?"

She says he left at about 4:30 to go pick up some shoes downtown. He was gone about an hour, she says, "because he come back at five." He stayed at her place until 8:00. She knows this, she says, "because I asked him to go to the store, you know, to get me a *TV Guide* and get me a beer."

The *TV Guide* will prove pivotal to this testimony.

I'm not in the courtroom, but I when I read the transcript later, I have a vision of Levenberg slowly stalking the young witness.

He knows something about her: She is on welfare and her boyfriend lives with her, and that makes her ineligible for the welfare. Levenberg has told my husband he's going to bust her there on the stand and get her kicked off welfare. When I hear about his plan, I hate Levenberg even more. The tactic feels sleazy, like he's cheating to win by taking advantage of her poverty. As it turns out, he doesn't have to use his trump card.

He begins his cross-examination asking her where she lives, and who lives with her.

"Me and my son," she says.

"No one else lives at that address?"

They go around that question a few times, with the witness maintaining that her old man lives in East Cleveland with his mother.

Then Levenberg gets lucky. He asks her on what date she last saw David Francis.

"July ninth," she says, the date he raped me.

They discuss the shoes, and the *TV Guide*, and the beer. The witness explains that she asked Francis to get the *TV Guide* for her because her old man was over at a neighbor's, getting a skillet.

"You don't remember what day of the week that was, do you?" Levenberg asks.

They say lawyers should never ask questions without knowing what the witness will answer, but I think her answer surprises even the wily Levenberg.

"I think it was a weekend," she says. "Yes, it had to be a weekend because he was going to get me a *TV Guide*, which was Friday. Right. Friday, that is when they come out."

"And you needed a new *TV Guide*, right?"

"I get them every Friday."

July 9 was a Monday.

The judge sends the jury to lunch. After they leave, the public defenders immediately ask for a bench conference.

"I just want the record to reflect this," one of them tells the judge. "In my professional judgment and opinion, the testimony that was just elicited from this witness, and that which I intend to put on from the next witness, I can't vouch for the credibility of these people at all. I am only putting them on because my client has instructed me to do so."

The second alibi witness leaves the Justice Center and does not come back. David Francis does not testify. The defense rests its case.

In the closing arguments, which I am allowed to see in court, one of the defense lawyers drops the suggestion that the first time I saw the "DAVE" tattoo was when I saw David Francis in the lineup. Levenberg erupts at that one when his turn comes: "Unless I missed something here entirely, that information about the tattoo was provided to the police department on July ninth, 1984!"

When the jury files out, Levenberg tells us not to worry, that it's done, we won. I worry for the entire hour the jury deliberates. Their verdict: Guilty on all eighteen counts.

The next day, Friday, October 26, Judge Hanna sentences Francis. I sit in the courtroom between my husband and my mother, gripping their hands. Francis clicks his tongue once or twice and refuses to speak when the judge gives him the opportunity, but instructs his lawyer to say that he is innocent and he will appeal. Of course he will. This will never be over.

The judge looks at me for several moments, and then turns to Francis.

"Those of us who believe in God and try to live by God's law are also taught to try to see the Lord in all of his creatures," he says. "In this position, that is getting increasingly harder. Today with you, Mr. Francis, it is nearly impossible. It is an evil and vile thing you did. Fortunately for her, and unfortunately for you, you picked on a woman who had the courage to fight back and stand up to you and prosecute you, so that at least she has spared the July tenth victim that you were looking for, and all of the other victims that you may have looked for, because there will be none. She prosecuted you, the jury convicted you, and for my part, sir, I shall bury you in the bowels of our worst prison for as long as I can."

He sentences Francis to thirty to seventy-five years. "I hope I am giving you a life sentence," Hanna says, "because that is what you deserve. And if I am not here in twenty years when you go before the board, these words will be. They will be part of your file. That is all."

★

I did not look at David Francis after the judge spoke. But now I know he looked at me. When I went through the prosecutor's files in 2007, I found a report from the sheriff's deputies who guarded him during the trial. It was just one page, unmarked and loose in the stack of papers, like an afterthought.

"He stood and looked in the direction of the victim and said, 'Yeah. Go ahead and celebrate. Pass out cigars,'" the report read.

He must have mumbled; I didn't hear him. The deputies told him to sit down.

"Some moments later," they reported, "the defendant, David Francis, again turned around to face the victim and stated, 'I'm gonna fuck you up.'"

CHAPTER FOURTEEN

"Once in a while I think of things too bad to talk about"

David Francis was true to his word. He did fuck me up. Not that I recognized it. I thought it was all over, that he was gone for life.

I was determined not to play the self-pitying victim, that despised female role that the writer Leslie Jamison describes as "The Girl Who Cried Pain," so I wore the costume of a woman who had never been a victim, never been raped. I had strength and resilience. I was Woman. Hear me roar.

If I got depressed sometimes, well, didn't everybody?

★

I had a pattern. One day, for no reason I could ever discern, I would awake filled with foreboding. A gloom would slip over my spirits—just a shadow at first, easy to deny. Over the next few days, the shadow would grow deeper. I would carry on, acting as though all was well. But all was not well. I would feel the way I felt as a child when I walked home from a friend's house at dinnertime, the sky turning dark. I'd look into the windows of the houses I passed, catching glimpses of mothers cutting onions or stirring something on the stove, kids doing their homework at the kitchen table, fathers watching the news in the living room. From the outside, those lighted windows looked like pure happiness, yet they brought on a feeling I couldn't name until much later. Melancholy.

When I admitted to myself that I was depressed, again, I would find a therapist, go for three or four sessions, talk about my childhood and my marriage and my stressful job but gloss over the rape—"I got over it," I insisted—and then abruptly stop going when the therapists suggested otherwise. When they wanted to prescribe antidepressants, I refused. They scared me.

In between therapy attempts, I pushed against the depressions with restless activity. I couldn't curl up in bed and give in to them: I had two children, I had a job with daily deadlines, we owned a house that always needed something repaired, usually something expensive. I drove to doctors' appointments and hockey practices and dance classes. I attended school parents' nights and volunteered in my children's preschool and elementary school classes. Once a month, I prepared healthy afternoon snacks for those classes. I bathed my children in oatmeal when they had chicken pox. I bought poster board and felt markers for school projects, and helped my son set flame-resistant baby clothes on fire for a science fair experiment. I decided to completely gut and renovate my kitchen. I kept myself so busy with ordinary life and insane home improvement projects, I didn't have time to resolve anything about David Francis for the next two decades.

He and the rape remained where I left them, buried and secret, until the next depression arrived, the next three sessions with the next therapist, the next time I had to tell the story to someone new.

★

After the trial, I went to the second therapist in my string of therapists. This therapist saw both my husband and me, but separately, and had me take several psychological tests. The only one I remember clearly was the Minnesota Multiphasic Personality Inventory, a test that makes you answer "true" or "false" to statements like, "I am very seldom troubled by constipation" and "Once in a while I think of things too bad to talk about." When I came to that one, I wanted to write in: "Only once in a while?"

As a student at the University of Minnesota, where the MMPI was developed in the late 1930s, I was automatically part of the ongoing control group and had to take it fairly often, often enough to remember that it focuses on the frequency, consistency, and color of one's poop with the fervor of a toddler during potty training, though without the giggles.

The therapist wrote up a five-page report on the tests and her impressions, which I discovered not too long ago in an old box of files in my attic.

"Shortly after the rape occurred," she wrote, "Ms. Connors stated that she felt she had completely lost control of her life.

She experienced ringing in her ears, dizziness, and an inability to concentrate on her work. Further, she panicked when she had to be alone, and she often retreated from her husband and spent much time curled up in a fetal position."

I don't remember the ringing-in-the-ears part, or the dizziness, but the difficulty concentrating on my work—or on anything else—endured. Part of this undoubtedly came from having children, who want your attention all the time, and part from the steady encroachment of technology, which also wants your attention all the time. But it started with David Francis.

After seeing my husband, the therapist wrote that he said my personality had radically changed. "The Joanna who went into that theater is not the one who came out," he told her. He said he felt he had lost his wife.

The therapist quotes me saying, "I just felt like I would never be happy again. I wasn't considering suicide or anything, which is what everyone was trying to intimate very subtly." Who was "everyone"? I'm not sure. My husband? My family?

Maybe I was the one doing the hinting, subconsciously. Because I did think about suicide, even though I told no one. I lied to that therapist and all the therapists who would follow over the years.

They asked about it right away, usually framing it as "Are you thinking of hurting yourself?" For some reason, the word "suicide" was taboo. I always said no. Doesn't just about everyone say no? How many people would be committed to institutions right now if we all gave the honest answer? Which was, for me and probably for a lot of other people: "Sometimes, yes. Sometimes I do think about it."

When I thought about suicide, I was taking my part in the retelling of an old story. Livy, in his massive *The History of Rome*, recounts the story of Lucretia, a noblewoman of the sixth century B.C. who was known for her great virtue.

Lucretia was married to a soldier who liked to brag about his wife. Around about 510 B.C., he told some of his fellow soldiers that his wife's virtue was purer than any other wife's in Rome. With this challenge laid down, the men rode to Rome to check her out. There, they spied upon Lucretia and her handmaidens spinning wool. The sight of Lucretia was too much for Sextus Tarquinius, a soldier and the son of the tyrannical seventh king of Rome, Lucius Tarquinius Superbus. A few days later, Sextus snuck back to Lucretia's house and threatened to kill her if she did not succumb to him.

When the rape ended, Lucretia told her husband and father what happened, fell to her knees, cried for vengeance, and plunged a dagger into her heart. Legend, or history, says that her rape and suicide sparked a revolt against the tyrant king, which led to the creation of the Roman Republic.

I wasn't thinking about suicide, and I was thinking about it. The way I put it to myself was: I can see why other people do it. I can imagine what a relief it would be. That's what suicide seemed to me: a relief. No more fretting. No more waking up with my heart thumping so high in my chest it seemed to have migrated to my throat. No more nightmares, with DAVE slipping into my room and putting his hand over my face. No more leaden days in bed, listening to the clock ticking the seconds to evening.

With one therapist, I ventured to go beyond my standard "no" and say that I could see why other people commit suicide.

She asked if I had a plan, and I said, "No. No, of course not." Again, doesn't everyone say that, even—especially—the ones who really do have a plan?

But I did think about how I would do it. Sort of.

I thought about it mostly when I swam. I went to the pool at Cleveland State University almost every day, escaping the newsroom for an hour to be alone in the water. I had been swimming laps for years so I wouldn't get fat, but now swimming did something else for me. It offered a retreat from the world that felt almost sacramental.

I don't think it's a coincidence that so many religious rituals involve water. Christians wade into rivers for baptism, Catholics dip their fingers into holy water as they enter the church, Jews go to the *mikvah* for purifying baths, Muslims wash before the five daily prayers, Hindus go to the sacred Ganges. Immersing yourself in water is like praying. It's a surrender, an elemental act that is the closest we humans can get to returning to where we started, curled up in our watery maternal bath, submerged in both safety and oblivion.

Oblivion is what I was after. I always entered the pool at the deep, deep end, where the diving towers loomed above the deck, three levels of concrete as high as a circus trapeze platform. I never jumped into the pool. I eased myself in from the side, slowly, feet, ankles, legs, knees before finally letting go, dropping like a stone into the water. At first I swam fast to warm up, then I eased back a little, my strokes matching the rhythm of my breathing, the only sound the pool pump as it whooshed in and out, in and out, like a heartbeat, surrounding me, supporting me.

I could let go, I thought. Just sink down to the bottom of the deep end, drown myself in relief.

I didn't think further than that, in my delusional fantasy of escape. Drowning oneself isn't so easily accomplished, in the absence of injury or weights. The body overrules the mind and claws toward the surface, determined to save itself. Virginia Woolf had thought it through when she put rocks in her pockets to stay down.

The therapist prescribed an antidepressant. This was before Prozac came along, and I was afraid of the side effects of the early antidepressants doctors were giving patients. I didn't fill the prescription, I stopped seeing that therapist, and I never told another one that I understood the appeal of suicide.

With time, the thoughts went away on their own. Years later, I told my sister Nancy about my suicide ideations. "I guess I wasn't serious, but I really thought about it a lot," I said.

Nancy was the one who had to point out the flaw in my fantasy, a flaw so obvious it's remarkable I had never thought of it myself.

"Jo," she said, "I don't think the lifeguards would have just sat there and watched you drown."

★

Then, just like that, I began to pull my hair out.

I don't remember when I started, or how, but I do remember that it quickly became a habit that was hard to break. Every day I vowed I would stop pulling my hair, and every day I would find myself in the middle of it. I would be reading, or watching TV, and my fingers would begin to stroke my hair, combing through the thick locks, examining the different textures. I would carefully separate the wiry ones, select a strand and pull. It had to come out clean, not break off, and it was only satisfying if it hurt a little bit. The ritual, and maybe the pain, too, brought on a calming reverie. In an hour of reading, I often pulled hundreds of strands, dropping them on the floor beside me. Later, when I cleaned them up, the thick clump in my hand horrified me. But not enough to make me stop.

My hair has always been thick, so I thought the pulling was my humiliating little secret until the day my mother, who was visiting, stood over me at the dining room table and said, "Jo! You have a bald spot!"

I renewed my vows to stop. I gave myself stern talks and bought gloves to wear when I read. Nothing worked. When I realized I couldn't control this new compulsion, I did some research and discovered that hair-pulling is common enough to have a name: trichotillomania. Psychologists aren't entirely sure what causes it, but many believe it is a form of self-soothing stress relief related to depression, anxiety, and obsessive-compulsive disorder.

In an online search, I found a therapist who listed the compulsion as one of her areas of expertise. When I went to see her, though, I found myself too embarrassed to tell her why I was there. After she coaxed me into talking about it, and I heard myself describing the careful selection of each hair, the toying with it, the final tug, the whole ritual felt bizarre and sad.

We talked about my depression, my work anxieties, the panic I felt about my children, my extreme surveillance of their lives. I did not think to bring up the rape until the second session.

"But I got over it right away," I told her. "He went to prison, so I didn't have anything to worry about, and I went back to work. I was OK."

She was silent.

"And then I had the kids, so I was pretty busy," I said.

Still silent.

"I tried not to think about it."

She took my hand, something no therapist had ever done.

"I'm so sorry that happened to you," she said. "And I have to tell you, I don't think you got over it."

Without any buildup or warning, I started crying. I clutched her hand and sobbed.

She went through the symptoms I had described—the hypervigilance, the insomnia, the emotional avoidance and withdrawal, the occasional flights into disassociation—all of which, she added, had appeared after a serious trauma: the rape.

"This adds up to post-traumatic stress disorder," she said. "Your hair-pulling is another symptom. It's strongly related to PTSD."

I shook my head, still crying. "That can't be true," I managed to say. The PTSD I knew about happened to soldiers. To my mind, it belonged exclusively to combat veterans who lived through the waking nightmare of war, to men and women who had watched their friends die and expected the same for themselves. It belonged to heroes. It did not belong to a woman with a bald spot on her scalp.

The therapist suggested Prozac, which was fairly new at the time and thought to be helpful with obsessive-compulsive disorders. I had always said no to antidepressants, out of fear of the side effects. Weight gain. Sexual problems. Suicidal ideation. This time, though I was still reluctant, I agreed to take it. Anything to stop pulling my hair out.

Recent studies have suggested that Prozac and similar antidepressants do not help with trichotillomania. Perhaps not, perhaps it was purely placebo effect, but after a few months I stopped pulling out my hair, at least most of the time. I still fell into depressions, and my anxieties continued to flare, but the drug had the odd effect of flattening my moods much of the time. I wasn't "better"—I just didn't care as much about anything. My sister Nancy called it the "Que sera, sera" pill, which instantly put the sugary voice of Doris Day on a loop running through my brain: "Que sera, sera; What will be, will be; The future's not ours to see; Que sera, sera." I hear it every evening, when I shake the capsule into my hand and pop it into my mouth.

My PTSD was chronic, the therapist told me. I will always have to deal with it. Still, I didn't want my drug consumption to be lifelong. I've tried several times to wean myself off Prozac, without success. My insomnia returns, my nervous system goes into overdrive, I become touchy and irritable, and I experience strange symptoms: a metallic taste in my mouth, like I'm chewing on pennies, accompanied by random jolts all over my body that feel like tiny electric shocks.

I asked my therapist what I should do.

"If you were diabetic, would you decide you should be strong enough to go off insulin?" she asked.

CHAPTER FIFTEEN

Crossing the border

In July of 2007, I had finished reading every document and transcript that gave me an excuse to stay home. It was time to go out into the world and look for people who knew David Francis.

I still wasn't sure what I would find as I looked into my rapist's background. I wanted to know more about him, to answer the question "Why him?" But I wanted and needed more than that. I wanted meaning. Context. I wanted a narrative that would make sense of my rape and explain why David Francis found me that July day, what forces led us to that spot where we collided.

First I looked for his two alibi witnesses from the trial. They had moved or married and changed their names so many times, their public records trail led me nowhere. Social Security death records told me that David Francis's mother, Millie Francis, also known as Matia Rodriques, died in August of 1984, the month after her son raped me, and two months before the trial. She was sixty-four years old. Her boyfriend, Earlie B. Giles, died in 1999, when he was seventy.

Next, I went back through the parole reviews for David Francis, inmate #A181-778, who was up for parole in 1991, 1995, 1997, and 2000, all without my knowledge. The Ohio Department of Rehabilitation and Correction instituted a victim notification system not long after David Francis went to prison. The system contacted victims who had officially registered for it, and of course only victims in new cases were told it was necessary to register. The victims of criminals who were already in prison were never told we had to register, so we never knew when our perpetrators came up for parole.

The parole forms require the inmate to identify people who will help them in their post-prison "parole plan." Twice, David Francis gave the name and address of Ida Taylor, once saying she was his grandmother, the second time his aunt. I could not find a working phone number for her, so I would have to go into the Hough neighborhood to see if she still lived at that address.

It takes ten minutes to drive to Hough from Shaker Heights, a distance of a few miles that covers an enormous divide. The drive leads across the border of the America that Andrew Hacker called, in the title of his 1992 book, *Two Nations: Black and White, Separate, Hostile, Unequal*. It leads into the heart of the rust-belt city that the U.S. Census Bureau designated the poorest big city in America in both 2004 and 2006. In that poorest city, Hough is the poorest neighborhood.

Taylor's house is just three and a half blocks from 79th Street and Hough Ave., the corner that was the epicenter of the Hough riots in the summer of 1966—the decade of racial unrest and riots in America. It started outside the Seventy-Niners' Café when the white owner refused to give a black resident a glass of water, and then taped a sign to the door reading: "No Water for Niggers." The six nights of arson and violence that followed left four dead —all of them black—and dozens injured. Countless acts of vandalism and hundreds of fires devastated the already struggling neighborhood, which never fully recovered. The following year, Carl Stokes was elected the first black mayor of a major American city, but racial tensions did not go away. In 1968, riots erupted again, in the nearby Glenville neighborhood.

In 1981, fifteen years after the Hough riots, Cuyahoga common pleas judge Burt Griffin wrote in his book *Cities Within a City*, "Hough ranks near the top in all of Cleveland's disagreeable statistics—welfare recipients, crime, abandoned buildings, rate of illegitimate births and school dropouts."

By 2007, when I went to find Ida Taylor, I could see scattered signs of recovery. A few brand-new McMansions and rows of town houses occupied long-vacant lots, but they shared blocks with abandoned houses boarded up with plywood and lots filled with weeds and trash.

I was afraid to go into the unfamiliar area alone, so I called my friend Sue, a psychiatric nurse whose work took her into Hough and Cleveland's other poor and distressed areas every day. She made house calls to recently released patients from the city's public mental health hospital, cajoling them to take their medications. She routinely went beyond her official job description, though, giving her clients coats and clothes, or finding their long-lost relatives.

I once went with her on a Saturday afternoon as she tried to track down a set of dentures one of her clients lost when the police found the woman outside on a cold evening, naked and shouting, and carted her off to the hospital. The search ended when Sue took her client—who was not only toothless but blind—back to her abandoned house in East Cleveland and kicked in the door. I knew Sue would be game to go along on this venture of mine.

We drove into Hough on a bright Saturday morning, with me gripping the steering wheel of my minivan while Sue talked and laughed, reapplied her lip gloss a few times, and, in general, appeared to be on her way to a fabulous party. We pulled up to an enormous house, one of the many mansions built a hundred years back, when Hough was a swank neighborhood and still home to the city's haughtiest private boys' school. The school had long since relocated to Shaker Heights, and no one would call Taylor's home a mansion now. It needed a paint job, moss grew on the roof, the front porch slumped precipitously to one side. A planter in the bare front yard held plastic flowers. Sue told me to park across the street so we could watch the house for a while before we approached.

After ten or fifteen minutes, a stocky man walked up the driveway and went inside; a minute later, we saw him peering out at us from a front window. Sue decided we had to either leave or knock on the door—no more waiting. I chose the door.

I knocked and the man answered, opening the door just a crack. "What do you want?" he said. "I saw you over there in your car."

Reporters do this all the time, knocking on the doors of strangers they can't reach any other way, but I had never done a story that required it. I was lucky: Reporters hate doing it. It's scary and rude, and we know the intrusions are a major reason Americans have such a low opinion of the media.

The man standing in front of me was not making it easy. My nervous system revved into overdrive, ready for me to run.

"I'm looking for Ida Taylor," I said. "Does she still live here?"

He looked at me with suspicion and nodded.

"Is she home?" I asked.

"What do you want with her?"

"I'm a reporter for *The Plain Dealer*."

This was true and not true. At that point, in 2006, I was working on the story by myself, on my own time, not for *The Plain Dealer*.

I had told one trusted editor about it, an editor who had helped me move from reviewing movies to writing long-form journalism, but I had not asked for an official assignment because I wasn't sure this story, whatever it became, would fit the newspaper model.

I wanted to write about my rape in detail—detail no newspaper would print—to show that rape is not what most people imagine it is from watching movies. It is not dramatic, or exciting, and I was not "brave" during it, as so many people assured me I was. I was not brave afterward when I testified. I did what I had to do. I went through the motions required by both the rapist and the legal system. I was, in fact, a coward, living in fear of the death I had glimpsed.

So when the man at Ida Taylor's front door asked me what I wanted with her, I had a vague answer prepared, the answer I would give everyone I encountered as I went along.

"I'm doing a story on men who died in prison in Ohio," I said, "and I think she knew one of them."

True, but not the whole truth. I thought it would shut people down entirely if I said, "I was raped, I'm doing a story about the man who did it, and I know you knew him." So I came up with the "men who died in prison" explanation.

"Is she home?" I asked again.

He closed the door on me. It occurred to me that perhaps I shouldn't have mentioned prison.

I turned and fled, with Sue right behind. We were almost to the minivan when an older woman opened the front door. "Somebody want to speak to me?" she called.

Ida Taylor didn't ask questions after we introduced our-selves and I told her I was a reporter. She invited us in and led us to the living room, apologizing for how slow she was. Bad knees, she said. Arthritis.

She motioned for us to sit on the couch and eased her bulk into a chair across the room, beneath a framed portrait of Martin Luther King Jr. Next to him, someone had hung a pink Mother's Day card that was as big as a movie poster.

"What can I do for you?" she asked.

I told her I was looking for information about her nephew, David Francis, who died in prison. She looked puzzled.

"David Francis?" she asked. "Who's that?"

I explained about finding her name on the parole records.

"Oh, David *Francis*," she said. "Millie's son. He's not my nephew."

I knew from looking her up on Nexis that Taylor was seventy-one, but she seemed at least ten years older. She'd raised her ten children in this house, she told us, five Harrisons from her first marriage and five Taylors from her second. Grandchildren and friends had lived with her, too, over the years.

But David Francis? No, he never lived there. His mother Millie did.

Taylor said she met Millie back in the '70s, at a neighborhood after-hours joint that a woman named Velma Chaney ran out of her basement. Millie was new to Cleveland, and told Ida she was on the run from her husband back in Boston, afraid he would find her and kill her. She brought her two youngest children to Cleveland with her, and David showed up not long after that, on his own. Charlene, Millie's oldest, was married to a man from Cleveland and already here.

Taylor said she let Millie move into an upstairs bedroom when she was down on her luck.

"This house has had some of everybody living here," she said. "My kids come and go; grandkids. Long as you abide by my rules, I'll have you."

When she moved to Ida's house, Millie gave her two youngest children to Velma Chaney to raise. Taylor remembered that. It was sad. But she said she didn't really remember David. He wasn't around much.

She called into the dining room: "Do either of you remember David Francis?"

The man who answered the door appeared with another man, both of them eating burgers half-wrapped in bright yellow paper.

"David Francis?" the second one said. "No."

Taylor thought for a minute. "I remember now," she said. "They called me from the prison to say he died. It was years ago."

"He died in August of 2000," I said.

"I don't know why they called me," Taylor said. "But they said my name was in his file, and they wanted to know what I wanted to do with his body. I said, 'I couldn't tell you. All I know is, his mother is dead. His brothers and sisters are in Boston, but I don't know any of their numbers. You'll have to do with him what you do. I don't have the money to bury him.'"

She shook her head. "I hated it, but there was nothing else I could do."

Ida looked over at the men. "These are my sons," she said. "Russell and Gregory. Russell is the oldest of all my kids."

Russell, who wore a gold cross the size of an Olympic medal, corrected his mother. He was the *Reverend* Russell Harrison, he told us before settling down on the couch so close to Sue he was almost touching her. He gave her a sly wink and a "let me buy you a drink" smile.

Gregory, who had answered the door, was still suspicious of us. He sat down near his mother and stared at us, saying nothing, while Russell nudged closer to Sue.

"What's your name?" Russell asked her. "And tell me why I never met you before."

Sue looked at him and laughed. "Oh, please," she said. He laughed, too.

"Don't mind me," he said. "I just like the ladies."

Later, I would recognize Russell's name coming up, here and there, in David Francis's police records. Back in the '70s, they'd been arrested together a few times for breaking and entering.

Taylor, her memories coming back to her, said that Millie hooked up with Earlie B. Giles at the after-hours joint.

"Earlie B.," Russell said. "He the guy with one eye missing?"

Taylor nodded.

She said Earlie B. came with Millie when she moved into the house. "They stayed in their room most of the time and drank," Taylor said. "She was a stone alcoholic. And she had that crippling arthritis real bad. It was hard for her to go up and down the stairs."

In the summer of 1984, Millie's arthritis and the drinking got so bad, her oldest daughter took her back to Boston. A couple of months after that, Taylor heard she died in a house fire up there.

"She was in a wheelchair on the second floor," Taylor said. "She burned up. They say her husband set the fire, but no one ever proved it."

Taylor said she thought Millie's youngest daughter, Laura, still lived in Cleveland.

"I heard she got into drugs and was on the stroll," Russell said. "But I saw her about a year ago at the food bank down on Superior. She said she was a Christian now. She was going to a church up around there somewhere."

He couldn't remember the name of the church or where it might be. None of them knew how to get in touch with her, or with any of the kids who went back to Boston.

"I haven't thought about Millie or her kids in years," Ida said.

Later, I called my sister Nancy to tell her about Ida and the parole records and the two sons. "They remembered his mother, but they didn't remember him," I said.

"Wow," Nancy said. "What if it turns out that you're the only person left who does?"

CHAPTER SIXTEEN

"David was the biggest mystery"

In myths and legends, the fire-breathing dragon never has a family. The dragon always lives alone in a cave or on a mountaintop, and the person who sets out to vanquish him must first go through a dark forest.

My dragon had a family. My dark forest was a wilderness of databases and public records.

David Francis was one of eight children born in Boston in the '50s and '60s to Mildred (or Millie) Rodriques and Clifford Francis.

I discovered this on one of the dozens of prison reports stuffed into the prosecutor's files—reports that had so little cohesion over David Francis's sixteen years of incarceration in five different Ohio prisons that each one offered different, almost random information. On this one, David Francis listed his siblings' names: Charlene, Clifford Jr., Philip, Joseph, Linda, Neamiah, and Laura.

I already knew their mother died a month after David Francis raped me in 1984. A Social Security death record check showed that their father, Clifford, died in Roxbury, Massachusetts, in 1995. The same record said Clifford Jr. died in 1994, at the age of forty.

I searched for the other siblings on Nexis, where I found page after page of names matching "Linda Francis" or "Joseph Francis." The women could have married and changed their names as well, and Neamiah—the one name I had a hope of finding—was off the grid as far as I could tell. Perhaps he never registered for Social Security and never voted or drove or put his name to any of the other information sources culled by Nexis.

I thought about trying to find Laura, the sister the Reverend Russell Harrison had seen, in one of the scores of churches that lined Superior Avenue, but that would be like trying to find someone by checking every Starbucks in Manhattan on a Sunday morning.

I finally found Neamiah in the Cuyahoga County criminal records, under the misspelled "Nemiah Francis." His five arrests, between 1987 and 2005, all involved drug possession and abuse, making him a casualty of the War on Drugs, which statistics show was waged mostly on young men in poor black communities across America.

Neamiah's last known address, in 2005, was an overcrowded men's homeless shelter in Cleveland, the one place Sue told me she hated to go to see her clients. When I called the shelter, they said he was no longer there. He could have gone anywhere, they said.

My last stab was Charlene, the oldest sister. David Francis listed her as his backup support for parole, if Ida Taylor couldn't take him. He had listed her married name, Blakney.

I decided to go to Boston for a couple of days to see what I could find of the Francis family at the Massachusetts Registry of Vital Records and Statistics.

I ended up spending the day there, in an office park on the outskirts of the city, going through birth, death, and marriage certificates. Dates of birth are especially helpful in records searches, and the marriage and death certificates might give me leads, too.

I found that Mildred E. Morrell (not Rodriques, or Matia) and Clifford G. Francis were married on August 8, 1950, by a justice of the peace in Boston. Clifford was twenty-four and a truck driver. Mildred was thirty years old and a "stitcher," which meant she ran a sewing machine in a factory.

Mildred was also pregnant. A birth certificate showed that Charlene Francis was born four months later, on December 19, 1950, in Boston. It noted the parents' races: Clifford was "red," Mildred was "col." I found birth certificates for all of the other children except the two youngest, Laura and Neamiah. I was beginning to think I would never find them.

A death certificate for Mildred Francis, "AKA Matia Rodriques," said she had died of "smoke inhalation and severe thermal injuries" on August 16, 1984. The cause of the fire was "pending investigation." Her son, Clifford Francis Jr., died under suspicious circumstances, too, on January 27, 1994, of "multiple blunt trauma to face and forehead, struck by another person in a residence." The medical examiner ruled it a homicide. His death, like his mother's, was unsolved.

Another marriage certificate showed that Clifford Francis Sr. remarried after Millie died. He lived another eleven years, dying on August 24, 1995, of pancreatic cancer. By then, his racial category on his death certificate had changed from "red" to "American Indian."

★

In 2007, the *Plain Dealer*'s editor retired. The publisher surprised us all when he hired the first female editor in chief in the paper's 150-year history. In June, Susan Goldberg arrived and changed everything for me. Like all editors, she wanted to put her stamp on the paper and win prizes with important stories. When my trusted editor told her about a story I was pursuing on my own—the David Francis story—she called me into her office to tell me she wanted it for the paper.

I still wasn't sure I would find anyone in the Francis family, or that I could produce the kind of story I knew she envisioned: a prize-winner. All editors, no matter how much they deny it, want to win the big journalism awards. Neither of us mentioned it, but it was obvious, and it made me uneasy. I never saw myself as a winner. Most of the time, I still felt like an imposter in the newsroom.

But I needed more than weekends and evenings to work on it, and I needed an editor to help me find my way. We came to an agreement. My children and my husband would have full veto power over everything in the story. I would have six months—a rare luxury in the news business—and a photographer with me on all of my interview attempts.

At the first editorial planning meeting, I noted another newspaper rarity. Almost everyone around the table was a woman—the editor, the managing editor, the features editor who would be handling my story, the layout editor, the copy editor, and the photographer. I wish I had taken a picture to send to the guy who'd asked about the "pulchritude corner."

I told them I had eleven different addresses for Charlene, all of them listed in Nexis as current, and I'd located one of the brothers, Philip, in the Massachusetts state prison at Bridgewater.

We decided I would go back to Boston to talk to Charlene and Philip, and that the photographer, Lisa, would go with me.

Setting up an interview with an inmate is a long process with many steps, and back then it was usually conducted by letter, not e-mail or phone. Massachusetts required me to get permission to see Philip first from the head of the prison system, then from the warden. After they signed off, I wrote to Philip directly to ask for an interview, and waited while the letter went through the prison's mail inspections. Then I waited for him to respond, and for that letter to go through the process in reverse.

When Philip didn't respond, I wrote again, this time including a letter of agreement that he could just sign. A few weeks later I got it back, signed "PHILIP," in block lettering. Someone else had written in his last name. I set up an interview date with the warden, and in October Lisa and I flew to Boston.

We looked for Charlene first. Some of her addresses were in Boston, but most were in New Bedford, a town on the coast south of Boston that was once the hub of the whaling industry. Herman Melville had worked out of New Bedford as a whaler.

New Bedford was also the site of a brutal barroom gang rape in 1983, the rape at the center of the 1988 film *The Accused*. The title referred not to the rapists but to the victim, who was drunk that night and wore a skimpy outfit. Even the prosecutor, a woman, initially thought this meant she'd asked for it and could not possibly claim she was raped. The movie was a hit. Critics loved it; Jodie Foster, who played the rape victim, won an Oscar. Even so, I could never bring myself to watch it.

The morning after we arrived, Lisa and I stayed in the Boston area to check Charlene's addresses there. One led us to vacant lot that had become a neighborhood dump. Among the litter, a rusted grocery-store cart, tipped on its side, held some beer cans and a soggy piece of clothing.

Next door, two men were bent over the engine of a car. I asked them if they knew anything about the family that lived in the house that once stood there.

"They say there was a fire, but it was years ago," one of them said.

This was where Millie, the mother of David Francis and seven other children, died in 1984, trapped on the second floor in her wheelchair while smoke filled the air and the fire—rumored to have been set by her husband—burned on.

We drove on to Brockton and then Dorchester, where the family lived when David was growing up. Martin Luther King Jr. lived not far from them in Dorchester in the 1950s, when he was getting his PhD at Boston University. The Dorchester house had been torn down, and in Brockton the house was vacant.

We drove down to New Bedford in the afternoon, into neighborhoods that looked just like Hough in Cleveland. Abandoned houses covered with plywood and spray-painted graffiti shared blocks with homes families still occupied. It was a Saturday, but no one was outside. No kids played, no one sat on a porch to catch the last warmth of the day. At one of Charlene's many addresses, a row house, the front door hung open on one hinge. Inside we could see a few pieces of furniture and some clothes and toys on the floor, left behind when the last tenants moved out.

Lisa did the driving on that trip, and as we rolled through these clusters of poverty in New Bedford she pointed out that our rental, an ugly, elongated orange SUV, could be a problem. "It's a clown car!" she said. I laughed, picturing dozens of clowns emerging from the back, but Lisa was serious. She took photos of it and sent them to a friend.

I didn't know her before we started working on the story together, but on this trip we got on like we'd been friends for years. I'm solitary by nature and had not wanted anyone working with me at first. I didn't want to share any decisions or have to explain myself to anyone, and when the story became a *Plain Dealer* story I worried that they would assign a male photographer, to "protect" me. But I saw early on that Lisa was a perfect counterpoint to me: She laughed a lot, charmed strangers, and had the kind of carefree confidence I had always wanted. Now she wasn't quite as carefree.

"We're not exactly inconspicuous here," she said. This was indisputable. She had cameras and other equipment she lugged with her at each stop, afraid to leave it exposed in the back of the SUV.

For once, I was the one who was not afraid, which struck me as odd but fantastic. Even with Lisa beside me, I should have had that familiar, adrenaline-fueled queasiness in my gut. Instead I felt removed from what we were doing, as though I was watching myself impersonate a reporter in a movie about two gutsy women investigating a story. I'd found courage in the place I felt safest: my disassociated state.

When we ran out of addresses in New Bedford to check, Lisa pulled into a McDonald's parking lot to regroup. I had three phone numbers, two for Charlene that Nexis had listed as disconnected, and one I found online for a Willie Blakney, who may or may not have been related to her. Nexis was correct on the first two numbers. On the third number, a man answered. I told him I was a reporter, I was looking for Charlene, and that I was writing about her brother David.

"Where did you get this number?" he asked.

I told him I found it online. He said, "Uh-huh," in a way that told me he didn't believe me.

I asked again about Charlene. "Do you know how I can reach her?"

"I'll tell her you called, but I don't think she'll want to talk to you," he said, and cut the connection before I could thank him.

"I think that was her son, but I don't think he wants me to talk to her," I told Lisa. We sat in the car, wondering about our next step. I didn't want to call him back for more hostility. It looked like my only option, though. I could not return to the newsroom without finding and talking to Charlene.

A couple of minutes later, my cell rang. I answered to a woman crying.

"Do you know what happened to my brother?" she asked. She could barely get the words out. "I tried to find him. I knew he was dead, but I've never known what happened to him."

It was Charlene. After I told her that her brother had died in prison, and I was a reporter from Cleveland doing a story about men who died in Ohio prisons, she said she would talk to us. She gave us an address that was not on my Nexis list.

On the way, I told Lisa I wanted to bring some flowers to Charlene. After about ten minutes of driving around we came to a grocery store. When we went in, I could see that it was the kind of store that overpriced everything and sold bruised produce and bread past its sell-by date to poor people who had no other options for shopping. I didn't really expect it to have flowers, but it did, a little collection of plastic-encased bouquets in buckets off in a corner. I grabbed a thin bunch going brown at the edges and paid $10.

Charlene was waiting for us at her door on the second floor of an apartment building, sniffling into a wet tissue. I introduced Lisa, handed Charlene the pathetic flowers, and followed her to the dining room, where open moving boxes filled with clothes lined the walls. A dinette table sat opposite an aquarium without water, its light glowing on a collection of plastic coral and ocean plants. Above it hung framed school pictures and family snapshots.

"I'm so sorry about your brother," I said, as though he had just died. She put the flowers on the kitchen counter without comment, offered us water, and then sat across from me at the table.

Seeing her there, sitting in her apartment, I was excited and ashamed at the same time. I'd found David Francis's sister, doing investigative work I'd never before attempted, in a city I didn't know. I'd done it. My story was coming together, right here.

But I was lying to Charlene, taking advantage of her grief. I was afraid to tell her the real reason I wanted to know about her brother. Before I talked about the rape, I wanted to see how she talked to me, see if she was as hostile as her son had been on the phone. My hands shook just a little when I put a digital recorder on the table between us and hit Record.

Charlene looked at the recorder. Neither of us said anything.

Lisa filled the silence for me. "Wow, that's a big fish tank," she said.

"I had some goldfish, but they died," Charlene said, her voice flat. She had stopped crying. "So we gotta fill it up again." She made it sound like filling up that tank and buying goldfish would take more energy than she could ever muster. Lisa and I nodded, smiling.

There is something almost deranged about what journalists do, meeting a stranger and immediately asking questions about her life. I once toured the county mental health hospital for a story. A mild-looking man, dressed in street clothes, approached me. "How old are you?" he asked. "Have you ever had sex? Do you think you're pretty?"

"Don't worry about him," the guide had said. "He's harmless."

I always think of him at the awkward start of interviews.

"Look at all these pictures!" I said. (Here I pause to tell you that I cringe when I listen to these recordings and hear this enthusiastic woman—me—chirping inanities.)

"It's all my kids," Charlene said. "And my kids' kids."

"How many kids do you have?"

"Me? I have eight, and eleven grandkids. Soon to be twelve. I have a great-grandchild coming."

"Wow!" I said. Charlene had no comment to that.

"So, you were the oldest of your brothers and sisters, right?" I said.

"Yeah. It was me, then there was my brother Heavy—"

" 'Heavy'?"

"Well, his name was Clifford but we called him Heavy. He was murdered in Boston."

"Murdered?" I said. I had already seen that on his death certificate.

Charlene didn't stop to explain. "Then there was my sister Linda. Ummm. Who's next? It was Philip, Joseph, Laura, and Neamiah."

"What about David?" I asked. "Where was he in the lineup?"

"David was right after Linda. So he was like the fourth."

"Were you close growing up?"

"He was my favorite brother," she said, sniffling. "Yeah, we did everything together. Got in trouble together, got locked up together—we did a lot of stuff when we were little."

"Locked up for, like, serious stuff?"

"No, for stupid little stuff, like stealing candy. I never got into any serious trouble."

Her voice caught when she said, "Everybody thought we was twins, we looked so much alike."

I looked closely at Charlene. Twins? She did have her brother's eyes—eyes that were both watchful and utterly weary. If he had lived into his fifties, and not gone to prison, David might have looked like Charlene, who was now fifty-seven, with an ample body that had gone soft and round at the middle, a face etched with years of drugs and alcohol and trouble, and those big eyes that missed nothing. Even though she was crying off and on, she unnerved me. I saw David in her eyes.

I stole a glance at Lisa, who sat on the floor over by the aquarium, listening to us and smiling. She hadn't started taking photos yet. She didn't look scared in the least.

I took a deep breath and told Charlene that I was writing about men who had died in prison without a family, or anyone else to bury them. I was looking for those families. I told her I knew David had died of cancer in 2000, in a prison hospital, and was buried in a prison cemetery in Ohio.

She started crying again. "I wrote to him in prison. He wrote back and told me he had a little girl. The second time I wrote, they said he had been released. Next time I heard, he was in Lucasville [prison], and he wrote back saying he had Lou Gehrig's disease. Then they wrote me back saying he had been released, and that's the last I heard from him."

She got up and came back with a handful of tissues. "Last time I called the prison, they told me David had died and been buried. I said, 'You had all my information, why didn't you call me?' 'Cause I wanted my brother's body. They told me he was buried in some damn debt place, and nobody knew where he was at. I was pissed off and tried to sue them, but I couldn't find a lawyer to do anything about it."

Charlene had buried everyone else in the family. Her mother first, in 1984, after the fire. Then Heavy, murdered in 1994. Then her father, cancer in 1995. Then Linda. Charlene said she died when she was forty-two, but she didn't tell me the year.

"It was mesothelioma," she said. "They think it happened in the fire that killed my mother. She was living at Linda's house, and Linda was there and her lungs got burned or something." She sighed. "After my mother died, we all just stayed drunk. So me and Linda used to party all the time, and she started getting so she couldn't breathe."

Charlene stopped and wiped her tears. "That almost broke me, burying my sister. It was the hardest thing I ever had to do."

I was quiet. "It sounds like you've had to do a lot of hard things in your life," I said.

Charlene nodded. "I used to tell people this family was cursed."

Then she told me about all the curses of her childhood.

★

"Your daddy's a pimp."

Charlene was thirteen when another kid told her that after school. "I wasn't sure what it meant," she said. "I thought maybe it was cool, since my daddy always had lots of money and owned houses and cars and this and that." Then she found out what it meant. It meant that the other women who lived in their house—sometimes two women, sometimes three, with all their kids—worked for her father.

In Charlene's telling, Clifford George Francis emerges as a mythical figure, a colossus who stomped through the world, destroying the women and children who feared and despised him.

Charlene's memories emerged in the form that our brains store them—disconnected and random. She spoke with a stream-of-consciousness flow, and when I listened to the recording later, I realized that for almost an hour I did not ask her a single question. I barely made a sound, other than saying *"Really?"* or *"That's terrible."* I was like a child listening to a bedtime story, a story filled with witches and graveyards, bags of money and black magic, poison and murders. And, as in so many fairy tales, this one featured an evil spirit that took the material form of parents.

Charlene started with her father.

"When I was little, they used to call him T.C., for Top Cat. He used to take me to the pool hall, and he used to hit the street numbers all the time. I remember a couple gangsters coming and walking us home, 'cause he had won all this money. He had a bagful of money. That's when he bought the first house, and a brand-new Cadillac. Lime green. Three days after he brought it home, David stole it and tore it up."

T.C. weighed more than five hundred pounds, Charlene said. "He was huge. He told us he was a full-blooded Narra-gansett Indian. He and his brothers all had this long hair and this high-red skin. And he had Indian superstitions, like he wouldn't let anyone take his picture because he said it captured your spirit. It should have told you something when he drank the fire water that something was wrong with him."

His mother, their grandmother, was a witch. "She practiced black magic," Charlene said. "She had these bull horns over her front door, and she confessed to me, right before she died, that she had given her soul to the devil. She was a horrible person."

Prejudiced, too. She didn't like Millie or her kids because they were black. As a full-blooded member of the Narragansett nation, she looked down on them. Once she asked her youngest grandchild, Laura, "What color am I?" When Laura answered, "Black," she locked her in the basement for hours.

"I remember the day my daddy brought the first woman home," Charlene said. "I was seven or eight years old, and I was outside, jumping rope, when he pulled up with this lady in the car. He went inside the house, and I heard a lot of yelling between my mother and my father. That was the first time he hit my mother, far as I know."

The lady's name was Beverly, but everyone called her Mary. "She had a baby sister, Theresa. She was fifteen years old when he brought her home to the house. They lived with us."

Over the years, Beverly/Mary had five children and Theresa had three, Charlene said. T.C.'s older children must have moved on, and I knew that some of them, including David, went to juvenile detention. Even so, it was hard to imagine, all those children and mothers living together in one house. Charlene was on a roll, so I didn't stop her to ask how they managed this, or why Beverly was called Mary, or what their last names were.

"I thought how we lived was normal," Charlene said. Then the kid at school told her that her daddy was a pimp.

"So when I did find out what that was, I asked him, 'Why would you do that to my mother?' 'Cause he used to beat up my mother, beat up the other women. It was a big mess. I guess you would call us—what do they call it now?"

"Dysfunctional?" I guessed.

"Yeah," she said. "That's the word. We were real dysfunctional."

The other women never brought the johns back to the house, she explained. "They went out and did their stuff and brought their money back. I never seen any of the guys they went with. My mother didn't prostitute. She and this other woman, Mary, they'd go out and steal things for him—you know, get clothes, food, jewelry, all this other stuff—and bring the stuff back to him."

T.C. wasn't just big—he was mean, Charlene said, especially when he was drinking, which was most of the time. When he beat their mother, Millie, sometimes he made her children watch. He beat the other women. He beat his boys—Clifford, Joseph, David, Philip, and Neamiah.

Charlene paused for a sip of water.

"Oh God, he was real mean. He'd hang them up on hooks and beat them with belts, and kicked them. My brother Heavy had a broken hip for almost two years and nobody even knew it. He would walk funny and nobody knew why until they took him to the hospital. It wasn't broken, it was out of place, and it was due to him beating Heavy."

He didn't beat the three girls—Charlene, Linda, and Laura. But T.C. abused them in other ways. "He told us we were worthless, we were stupid, that we weren't nothing but a bedsheet for men," Charlene said. "He was cruel."

Once, she remembered, when Laura and Neamiah were still little, he told them to get dressed. "You're going to go talk to your grandfather now," he said.

"Granddaddy's dead," Neamiah said. They all knew this. T.C. didn't say anything, he just put them in the car and took them to a graveyard. It was dark out by then. He took them to their granddaddy's plot and left them there all night.

"Me being the oldest, mostly I ended up taking care of my brothers and sisters, because when they was down there drinking and fighting, I would take the kids upstairs and we'd sit in bed and I would try to read the Bible to them. I became their second mother, and after she died, they would come to me with their drama. I just took over the family."

She paused. "They left me to bury everyone."

There was more. When they were little, Charlene said, she would go without eating to make sure the other kids were fed. "My appetite still isn't normal," she said.

She remembers once all of them were together in a bedroom, plotting how to kill T.C. Charlene wanted to put poison in his food and watch him eat it. But David was the only one to act on his plot. "One time, he tried to murder my father," Charlene said. "It was funny as hell. He locked my father in a room and set the room on fire. He didn't die in it, he ended up jumping out the window, and David took off in the brand-new Cadillac. He was about twelve or thirteen. I didn't see much of David after that."

All five boys started getting in trouble around that age, Charlene said, mostly for stealing cars.

I knew from the records in the prosecutor's file that David had just turned twelve when he got the first entry on his rap sheet: an arrest for assault and robbery. His juvenile record from Massachusetts goes on from there, for pages and pages, fifty-three entries that record an adolescence of arrests for committing theft, breaking and entering, carrying concealed weapons, doing drugs, and escaping from detention. He was sent away most of the time.

The girls, too, got into trouble with the law, for drugs and prostitution.

"I was addicted to crack for about ten years," Charlene said. "My brother Heavy, he used to sell it. So we'd be at his house on Green Street smoking, and then we'd go to other people's houses, we'd start smoking. When Heavy died, I ended up doing it even worse. He was murdered. They said it was that Heavy stole some drugs from these guys in Boston, and like six guys jumped him and fought him. They never found who did it. Never. I don't think they looked too hard."

It took her grandson's dying for Charlene to get clean.

"Little Thomas was two years old," she said, tearing up. "We was all drinking and drugging, and me and the guy I was going with at the time got into a big fight. My daughter lived upstairs, and I lived on the second floor, and me being so drunk

I put a cigarette on an ashtray and left it on my bed and forgot about it, and we went into another room and we were fighting, and next thing I knew the whole mattress caught on fire."

The guy she was going with tried to take the mattress outside, but he couldn't get it through the door and the hall filled with smoke. Everybody got out of the house. Except Thomas. They were all running around looking for him, yelling. The firemen found him behind a chair. Apparently the smoke scared him so much he was hiding back there.

"I went to that funeral, and I looked at my grandson in his little casket, and I promised him I would never touch another drug as long as I lived," Charlene said, the tears spilling over and running down her face again. "And I haven't. I haven't even touched a drink. I don't even have feelings for it anymore. I used to crave it; I would get mad if I didn't have it. But now I don't care about it."

Charlene always thought the whole family would end up dying from drugs or alcohol. David was the only one who didn't seem to like it. When they all got to drinking, he'd just take off. Nobody knew where he went or what he did.

"Of all of us," Charlene said, "David was the biggest mystery."

He had this problem with rage, she told me. "He would get so mad, until he wanted to kill somebody. But the thing is, the madder he got, the calmer he would get. He'd start talking real soft and low, calm, and then you knew to get the hell out of the way."

When she said that, a shiver went through my body, starting in my chest. I can hear myself on the recording, my sharp inhale, in the silence that followed.

That's how he talked to me. Soft and low. Calm.

"When I get out, I will find you," he said, just like that. With a kiss.

★

Lisa, who had been sitting on the floor across the room, saw that Charlene's energy was fading. When the conversation came to a pause, she popped up with a big smile.

"Hey, Charlene," she said. "I'd really like to take your picture."

She made it sound like they were going to have so much fun together. I never managed to do that when I interviewed people.

Charlene surprised me. I thought she'd say no, but she stood and walked into her living room. Lisa pulled open the drapes, hoping for natural light. Charlene looked like I imagine I look when a camera is pointed at me.

"Laura's gonna flip when she sees this," Charlene said as Lisa's camera clicked. "I've never let anybody take my picture."

"Why not?" I asked, thinking that I should stop letting people take my picture, too.

"I guess because my father was Indian and we was raised like that," she said. The camera kept clicking. Charlene didn't smile.

One of Charlene's grandsons came in and asked about dinner. She told him she'd start cooking soon, and I said we should probably stop, for now. But I wanted to talk again, if she didn't mind.

Then I said yet another thing that makes me wince when I listen to the recording.

"Tomorrow is Sunday," I said. "Are you planning on going to church?"

Charlene said no.

"We could take you to brunch," I said, in that weird, enthusiastic voice.

Brunch. I rewind the recorder. *Really? Where did I think I was, in an episode of* Sex and the City?

Charlene laughed. Sort of. In the transcript of the interview, I wrote: "Hahaha."

"I'm happy with anybody who takes me anywhere," she said. "I would love it. Just get me out of here."

CHAPTER SEVENTEEN

"If I hadn't been so stupid"

Later, I tried to fact-check Charlene's stories, but reporting has its limits. Some of what happened in that house, away from the eyes of outsiders, was impossible to corroborate. But I found many of her claims backed up by criminal records, and some confirmed by other people.

For instance, Charlene told me that Philip—the brother in prison for rape—once got arrested for impersonating a doctor. "We called him 'Inspector Gadget,' because he was always making stuff up," she said, tickled by the memory.

I was dubious; it was hard to imagine any of the brothers going from car theft and juvenile detention to striding into a hospital in a white coat. But when I checked his multipage Massachusetts rap sheet, there it was: Philip was arraigned in Boston District Court on September 25, 1981, for "Impersonation: Practitioner of Medicine." He would have been twenty-three years old. His alias was Dr. Murray Everett.

It's hard to pin down black magic, even if you practice the black arts of unearthing elusive documents. But eventually three siblings—independently of one another—told me about the midnight trip to the graveyard. They told me about their father hanging his sons on hooks. They told me their grandmother was an actual witch, with sinister powers. I figured that even if these and the other implausible stories weren't exactly true, after a lifetime of repetition they were true to the family. They gave a narrative shape to the chaos of their childhood.

When we knocked on Charlene's door on Sunday morning, she was dressed to go out for brunch, in white pants, a canary-yellow top, and gold shoes. She wore bracelets, several necklaces, and earrings and had put on makeup. She looked younger and happier.

I wore jeans and a black T-shirt. When I told her she looked great, she said, "The last time I wore this outfit was to Heavy's funeral in 1994."

Even though she was dressed up, she wasn't sure about going to brunch. Her family was coming over later, and she had to get ready.

"On Sunday they all come around, all of them come up for dinner. We have a pretty close relationship now. The whole family, we're just now trying to get ourselves together. I guess because everyone has seen me staying sober, so they're all trying to walk away from it."

We decided to talk in Charlene's apartment. The flowers I had given her were in a vase on the table in the dining room. I sat down, embarrassed by them. Lisa tried to disappear on the other side of the room, as she had the day before, so she could take pictures without Charlene—or me, for that matter—getting self-conscious.

"I always figured if I was doing drugs, I wasn't hurting nobody but myself," Charlene said from the kitchen. "It wasn't bothering you; it was my money I was spending so what are you worried about it for? I was like, after I got sobered up, that's when I realized I did mess up my kids with it, 'cause they had to put up with me passing out on the floor, fighting, running back and forth to different drug dealers, and stuff like that. So I'm glad I got it straightened up."

She brought over two glasses of water and sat down. "I'm so tired," she said. "I couldn't sleep all night. I had nightmares. David was on my mind."

She said she had called Laura, in Cleveland, before she went to bed. Laura told her something new.

"She said that they had said David murdered someone, which I didn't know about. I have no idea what David did after he left Boston, but according to her, I guess he killed one of the guards in jail for trying to rape him or something. So it was a lot of mess that David had been through."

"Can you give me Laura's phone number?" I asked. "Do you think she would talk to me when I get back to Cleveland?"

Charlene read the number from her cell phone, then snapped it shut and leveled her gaze at me.

"Laura was surprised, just like I was, that they got a reporter up here that wants to do a story about David," she said. "She was like, 'Why would they do a story about David?' I said, 'I have no idea.'"

She paused, looking at me with an expression that made me nervous. I didn't say anything. I wasn't ready for this.

"I mean, there's a lot of guys that die in prison," she went on. "And most of them die violently. It seems strange that they would do a story about David."

I stalled. "Do you and Laura talk very often?" I asked.

She shrugged. "It's only been maybe three years since me and my sister have been back in contact. The whole family scattered, everybody was lost, nobody knew where anybody was."

Charlene said Laura mentioned their brother Neamiah, one of the lost. Laura said the last time she saw him, he was in jail.

"He's a bad heroin addict," Charlene said. "The last time I saw Neamiah he was a boy, and according to everybody now he's had a sex-change operation. So I wouldn't know him if I went up to him. They say he's calling himself Sherry now."

I tried to imagine an addict who lived in a homeless shelter being able to get a sex-change operation.

"One time, he was living with me, and I came home and here he was sitting at the kitchen table wearing one of my dresses," Charlene went on. "Which shocked me."

Now I tried to imagine a transvestite trying to live peacefully at a men's shelter, or in jail.

"Poor Neamiah," I said.

"My father screwed us all up," Charlene said. "He destroyed my whole family. He really did. I hated him. He turned my brothers into crooks and whatever else you want to call them. The girls were prostitutes. We were all on drugs and alcoholics. Two of my brothers turned out to be gay, one was murdered. Laura and I lost both our kids to foster care, my daughter was on drugs and lost her kids. And Philip turned out to be a child molester."

What?

"He molested my son," Charlene said.

"He did?"

"I always trusted my brother. We'd drink together. He'd bring over big bags of vodka, and we'd party. But I come to find out that while I was drunk, he was molesting my son."

She walked over to the family pictures hanging on the wall. I followed.

"Here's a picture of my son," she said. She pointed to a handsome, smiling young man.

"He was Philip's favorite, and I had no idea that he was taking him to gay bars and porno theaters and all this. Now my son is in prison for molesting. He exposed himself to his sister. They took him at twelve, they kept him until he was seventeen, and he was worse when he came back. He's twenty-two now, and he's been in and out of jail ever since. He's in prison now because he was going with a girl who said she was eighteen and she turned out to be fifteen. Philip messed him up, real bad."

We returned to our seats in silence.

"David, now, David was one of the nicest kids you'd want to meet," she said after a minute. "But Laura told me he grew up to be a real thug. He could get mean when he got mad, but the things Laura was telling me last night, that just didn't sound like my brother. She said he tried to make her go out on the corner and work, he was trying to force her into prostitution, and that's just something I don't believe he would do, because David was always protective of his sisters."

Charlene stopped talking. I took a sip of water and cleared my throat.

"So," I said. "I have to tell you something. I really am a reporter, and Lisa really is a photographer for the paper, and I really am doing a story about David. But I've been waiting to tell you this until I knew I could trust you. I wanted to see if you were a nice person, a compassionate person, and I think you are."

She nodded, but I could tell I was confusing her with all this windup.

"The reason I'm doing the story about David is because I was his victim," I said.

"You? What do you mean, his victim?"

"He went to prison in 1984 for rape," I said. "I was a reporter back then, too, and I went into a building for work, and it was empty, and he had wandered in, and he had a knife, and he cut me and attacked me and raped me."

Charlene said nothing. I said nothing.

"Are you sure?" she asked at last.

"Yes," I said. "He had a tattoo of his name on his arm."

Silence. She looked down at the table, not at me. When she spoke next, her voice was quiet.

"I can't believe it," she said. "That just doesn't seem like my brother. David was—I never knew David even to treat women badly. He always had respect for women. I don't understand."

She looked at me, trying to make sense of what I had told her. "David was good-looking," she said, as though I might confirm this. "I mean, he had girlfriends; he didn't have trouble getting girlfriends. He didn't need to rape nobody."

I didn't want to get into a discussion of why men commit rape, so I filled the conversational gap with some history. I told her David was in prison—in Lucasville, the one she mentioned—when he was diagnosed with Hodgkin's disease. I said they let him out on a mercy parole because they thought he would die soon. Seven days after he was paroled, he raped me.

Charlene was sobbing by this point. "I don't understand this. I don't believe it."

After all the horrors she had described to me the day before, I was genuinely surprised this upset her so much. Her reaction raised troubling questions that I'd managed to push aside, questions of exploitation and appropriation that often lie at the very heart of journalism. Janet Malcolm, in *The Journalist and the Murderer*, wrote: "Every journalist who is not too stupid or full of himself to notice what is going on knows that what he does is morally indefensible. He is a kind of confidence man, preying on people's vanity, ignorance, or loneliness, gaining their trust and betraying them without remorse."

This quote offends many journalists. The first time I read it, I felt a sting of recognition.

I tried to explain why I had come to her with the news that her brother was a rapist. I stumbled through it. "The rape made me a different person, Charlene. It changed my life. I was thirty years old when it happened, and since then I've been afraid of so much. I've lived in fear for twenty-four years."

She wasn't looking at me. I wasn't sure if she was listening.

"A while ago I decided that the way to overcome your fear is to find out about your fear, what's behind it. So I decided to find him. And when I found out that he had died of cancer in prison, I decided to find his family."

Charlene was shaking her head.

"And I came to Boston and found you," I said.

She looked at me.

"Was he raping other women?"

I had wondered that, too. "I don't know," I said. "I didn't find any other arrests for rape."

She didn't respond.

"You know," I said, "when it was happening, I remember thinking, *He's doing this because someone did it to him.* That's what I thought."

"Well, Laura did say he killed somebody in prison for trying to rape him," she said.

"I didn't find anything like that in his record," I said. "No murders."

"I know he was capable of murdering somebody," she said. "He had that thing, that uncontrollable rage. So yeah, if you had come to me and said, 'Yeah, I'm here doing a story because David killed two or three people,' that would have made more sense to me than him being a rapist. He was always good to women. Women liked him."

She sighed. "I don't know what happened to my brother."

"That's what I wanted to find out," I said. "Because I had this sense that he had been a victim in some way."

"Well, we all became victims. None of us came out normal, every one of us had problems. But I never heard any stories of my brothers raping anybody. I mean, except for Philip, and he was molesting kids."

"Well, that's the thing about your son," I said. "They say a lot of molesters were molested by someone when they were kids."

Charlene cried again, thinking of her son. He was such a sweet little kid, she said, and they put him away so young, and then he came out a different person. She worries about what's happening to him in prison. She worries all the time.

We sat at the table, quiet, our worries and fears exposed and spread out before us.

Charlene was not finished, though.

"I know about rape," she said. "I was raped myself. Three times. But I asked for it, because I was on drugs and I was prostituting. And I never reported it to the police because, 'Hey, what the hell, you're prostituting, what do you think you're supposed to get?'"

"Charlene, wait," I said. "You didn't deserve it."

I was saying to her what others had said to me, but in her case I believed it: "It wasn't your fault. You didn't deserve it. No one asks to be raped."

Charlene shook her head.

"One of the times, I was high on drugs, and I went out to get more money to get more drugs," Charlene said. "This guy promised to give me fifty dollars if I gave him a blow job. So I got in the car with him, and instead of paying me he raped me and beat me and threw me out the car. And I couldn't go to the police because I was terrified. They wouldn't believe me because I was a drug addict. I mean, they didn't even give a shit about my brother when he was murdered, so why would they care about me?"

She looked up.

"And besides that," she said, "he was a white guy."

For Charlene, this was the final and most indisputable evidence that she'd asked to be raped, and that the cops would at best dismiss her claims and at worst arrest her.

There was so much I could have said about this, so much history and injustice and raw truth embedded in those four words—"he was a white guy"—but I didn't. Instead of reminding her of what female slaves endured from white owners for so long, or talking about how American laws did not protect black women from white rapists during Jim Crow, I said nothing. I'd like to think that I was focused on listening to Charlene like a good journalist, with attention and without interruption, but as I listen to the tape I know something else was going on.

I felt shame when she said that. I feel shame now, when I play the recording, and I still don't know what to do with it. By accident of timing and birth, and nothing more, I could report my rape without fearing that the cops would only make it worse. Charlene was, as James Baldwin wrote, "born into a society which spelled out with brutal clarity, and in as many ways as possible, that you were a worthless human being."

"God, I'm so sorry that happened to you," I finally managed.

"The second time, I walked right into it," Charlene went on, echoing what I always told therapists—and myself—about my rape.

"I went into a house to get high," she went on. "And it was a bunch of Puerto Rican guys, three of them. They raped me and beat me up and threw me out the house, naked. I didn't go to the police then, either."

"I'm so sorry."

"I asked for it," she said, sobbing again. "If I hadn't been so stupid."

Stupid. Stupid, stupid, stupid, stupid, stupid. We'd ended up in the same place, lashing ourselves with the same word.

"That's what I've been saying to myself for twenty years," I said. "I was so stupid."

"Yeah, but you weren't out there hooking for drugs," she said. "It's different. I mean, you had a good job and my brother had no right to do that to you, he had no right to do that to any woman."

I knew a lot of people would agree with her, including many cops and prosecutors: If you're a hooker, you can't say you were raped. If you're on drugs, you deserve whatever you get.

Even Charlene believed this. I had a job. I had an education. I had a husband who did not hit me. I had parents who did not hit me. She had lived with abuse and violence all her life. And still, she thought it was fair to say that what happened to me was worse.

"Charlene," I said. "They had no right to do what they did to you."

She wiped at her tears again.

"It's terrifying," she said. "Especially when you think they're going to kill you."

I nodded, unable to speak.

CHAPTER EIGHTEEN

"I try to wipe it from my memory"

Philip Francis was thirty-nine years old in 1999, when he was arrested for raping his nephew. He spent almost four years in jail, awaiting a trial, before he agreed to plead guilty in November of 2003. The judge sentenced him to four years, ruled that he had served the time, and released him on three years' probation. But Philip failed to register as a sex offender, one of the terms of his probation, and was back in custody in April of 2004. He had been in various state hospitals and prisons ever since, awaiting some resolution, when I went to see him at Bridgewater in the fall of 2007.

Bridgewater, a large complex of state prisons and lockup treatment centers south of Boston, became infamous for two things. In 1967, Albert DeSalvo—the Boston Strangler—confessed to raping and killing thirteen women and was sentenced to life in prison at the Bridgewater State Hospital for the criminally insane. Not long after he got there, DeSalvo escaped. He left a note for the hospital superintendent that said he had escaped to draw attention to the terrible conditions at the hospital. He gave himself up the next day.

The conditions De Salvo wanted to make public were revealed in the film *Titicut Follies*, a documentary by Frederick Wiseman that was released the same year DeSalvo escaped. Named for the annual show the inmates put on, *Titicut Follies* included shocking scenes of abuse, neglect, and the stripping and bullying of inmates. After it screened at the 1967 New York Film Festival, Massachusetts won an injunction banning its further distribution, citing an invasion of the privacy of the inmates. It was not until 1991 that a judge allowed the film to be shown to the general public. It included a postscript that said conditions at the hospital had improved since 1967.

The prison complex has four units for inmates: Bridge-water State Hospital for mentally ill offenders and defendants who need competency evaluations; a substance-abuse unit; a minimum-security prison; and the Massachusetts Treatment Center, a unit for sexual offenders like Philip. A prison spokes-woman directed us there, and after we went through the usual searches and checkpoints and locked gates, a guard led us to a conference room set up for a large meeting.

When Philip entered the room, he did not look at us. He had agreed to the interview weeks ago, but now his body language was reluctant and defensive. He shuffled over to a chair, his head hanging low, his gaze on the floor. He did not raise his head when he sat down, but stared at the table. The guard made sure he was settled and then stood at the door, his face impassive.

Philip was here because he had raped a child, but when I turned on the digital recorder and began asking him questions, I felt only pity for him. His answers were slow and halting, and his mouth couldn't quite form the words he was trying to get out. I wondered if he'd had a stroke or if something was wrong with his tongue. When he at last finished a thought and got it out, he punctuated it with a bark of a laugh that had no mirth in it at all. He was like a child himself.

Philip was fifty-one years old when I interviewed him. He had spent much of his adolescence locked up, and when he wasn't in prison he'd had to choose between surviving on the streets or going home to a father who beat him. As he spoke, I could see that he was missing many of his teeth.

I asked him about his father.

"He was a very angry person," Philip said, "but what he was angry about I don't know; I never really talked to him about it. The last time I seen him was close to when he was dying. I was in my twenties at the time. And he was all, 'I'm sorry for what I did, I never was a father and I can't blame you for hating me.'"

"Did you forgive him then?"

"I guess I tried. I guess so. I mean, I couldn't forgive him for the way he made my life turn out, but for the alcohol and the punishment, I forgave him for that."

I asked if it was true that his father was a pimp, as Charlene had told me, and he said, "I don't know about that. He had three different women in the house, and all their kids, but I don't know what-all they did."

"How did he make money to support you all?" I asked. "Did he have a regular job?"

Philip barked a laugh. "When I was nine or ten years old, I was hit by an ice-cream truck," he said. "And we won a lawsuit, and my father lived off that money; he got the ice-cream truck, too. I was in a body cast for maybe two or three years, and I suffered some head injuries. And then, like, six months after I got out of the cast, I started getting into trouble. Stealing cars, hanging out with hippies, drinking, doing LSD and all that. Windowpane, mushrooms. We used to hang out in Cambridge up at Harvard Square. I actually hung out with Janis Joplin up there."

"Really? Janis Joplin?" I hear in my voice the same astonishment as I do on my recordings with Charlene. "How old were you?"

"I was about twelve, twelve and a half at the time."

"Charlene said your father beat you and your brothers, and your mother, but not the girls."

"Yeah. He spent a lot of time drinking," Philip said. "He'd come home and drink and get in fights with my mother. We'd come home from school and he would beat us with bullwhips. I hated to come home from school. I would go as slow as I could go. He used to hang us in closets, stuff like that. On hooks."

When I asked about David, Philip smiled and barked out his laugh again, but with his eyes focused on the table. "David was my big brother and maybe my best friend. He was nice to me. He gave me my first drink and my first cigarette. I was, like, five and he was six. We snuck into my father's liquor cabinet and got drunk on vodka and beer." That laugh again. "Very drunk."

David also provided Philip with his introduction to crime. "We started stealing when I was maybe about ten, me and David," he said. "We used to steal Kool cigarettes (the nonfilters) radios, watches, and things. Back then they didn't have things locked up, so it was easy to walk into Woolworths and steal stuff."

"What happened when you got caught?"

"I mainly grew up in the DYS," he said. He was referring to the Massachusetts Department of Youth Services, a notation I had seen dozens of times on both brothers' criminal records. "I was in a special hospital for kids, 'cause I was suicidal, and I tried to kill my friends." Another laugh.

Charlene had spoken this way, too, injecting an offhand reference to abuse, or criminal activity, or even death. For instance, Charlene told me that she married when she was sixteen because she was pregnant and desperate to get away from her family. She didn't love her husband, but she moved to Cleveland with him. He turned out to be as abusive as her father. "And I just got tired of it," she said, "and one night I just stabbed him in the back and got on a bus back to Boston." She would have gone on to something else if I had not stopped her to ask if she killed him or been arrested. "No," she said. "He didn't come after me, either."

Another time, she spoke of her mother's last months in Cleveland, when she lived with Earlie B. Giles at Ida's house. "She was drinking all the time then, and whenever she needed money, she'd sell his eye," Charlene said.

Again, I asked her to stop and explain.

Earlie B. had a glass eye, Charlene told me. She didn't say why he had it, but what he did with it was the point of the story. He would take it out sometimes and leave it somewhere and then have to go looking for it.

"In Cleveland back then, you could pawn anything at the pawnshops," she said. "Nobody should have told my mother that, 'cause she stole his eye and went and pawned it so she could buy alcohol. So we're getting drunk, and Earlie B. comes in their room and he's missing his eye, and she told him what she did. It was funny as hell. Then after that, every week, when she needed money for a drink, she'd steal his eye and go pawn it." She laughed. "We had a good time in Cleveland. It was a party town back then. I miss my mother." Then she laughed affectionately. I laugh, too, every time I read the transcript.

★

I asked Philip to tell me about the suicide and murder attempts when he was young.

"I was in a place called Lyman School," he said.

I looked it up later. Lyman School for Boys, in Westborough, Massachusetts, was the first reform school in the United States. It opened in 1886 and closed in 1971. The Boston Strangler went to Lyman when he was twelve. Former residents have reported harsh rules and physical abuse at the school, and a few have alleged that the "masters" raped them while they were there.

Philip told me he was raped by a teacher, a man who, he said, preyed on the young boys in his charge without anyone but the boys themselves knowing about it.

"It's a big place, so most of the time he would take the kids up into the music room when no one was there."

"You didn't report it to anyone?"

"Who? He was in charge. I guess from that time on, I've kind of been suicidal. I've OD'd, I've slit my wrists, I've swallowed pills."

He said he was fifteen or sixteen when he left Lyman and went to a group home. "And then the group home closed down and I ended up in the streets. I saw my stepmother, Mary, and she said, 'Come live with us,' so I went, but then my father started on me again, so I left and I ran away from home again. I stayed in abandoned buildings; I would break into cars and stay in cars."

Philip told his story in disjointed episodes, each marked by either the prisons and juvenile facilities where he was sent, or by the things he did that got him to those places.

"For some reason I happened to be in my sister's house and I tried to kill the whole family," he said, out of nowhere. "I turned on the gas. That's why they sent me to another hospital. They said, 'You're a hard case to figure out because you have a habit of closing people out and you hear voices, and you stabbed a guy twelve times and you didn't even know you stabbed him.' They said it happened in downtown Boston. I don't remember it." The stabbing did not turn up on his criminal record, either.

I asked him about his nephew. "What happened there? Charlene said you molested him."

"I guess my nephew got in trouble, and he made some allegations that I supposedly had sexually assaulted him. I kept telling the DA I never touched him. He never mentioned it to anyone until he got in trouble. So I waited in jail like four years, waiting to go to trial on this case. And the DA said, 'Look, we'll let you go home if you plead guilty. There'll be no charges, nothing, you can go home.' I agreed. So I was on the street, I didn't get in no trouble. And because I don't write that good my probation officer was [in charge of] registering me as a sex offender, and I guess she forgot [to] and I got picked up for failure to register, and I went to jail for that." Three years later, he was still in prison.

As with Charlene, I didn't know how much of Philip's story was true. Memory is the ultimate unreliable narrator. Brain researchers theorize that what we think of as solid and immutable memories are actually fluid, changing slightly each time they are recalled. The more we tell the stories, the more they change, and with every telling the new, rewritten memory becomes the one we think we've always had.

The Francis family's stories also operated on the fuel of rumor and hearsay. The elusive "they" were always saying that someone killed someone in a bar, or someone got mad and stabbed someone, or someone died in a fire, or a fight. All of this went into their collective memories.

I asked Philip, "When did you last see David?"

"I don't know," he said, rubbing his eyes. "He was hanging with a bunch of people. He told me he was staying in Dorchester. That was about it. The next thing I know, I heard he was locked up for killing some cabbie here in Boston. I guess him and his buddies, they robbed some cabdriver and killed him, and David turned state's evidence, because the next thing I heard he was in Ohio."

Philip had started crying.

"I spend a lot of time crying," he said, swiping at his face with his bare hand. "I try not to reflect too much about growing up; I try to wipe it from my memory. Because I don't think any child should have to suffer like that. Especially for something they didn't do. Like I tell my psychiatrist, it's not my fault I was born, I didn't ask to be born, and I don't know what would possess any man to hurt a kid like my father did. Especially his own family."

For the first time that afternoon, he raised his head and looked at me. "I still try to figure it out to this day," he said. "What did we do wrong to deserve such a tragic life? You know?"

CHAPTER NINETEEN

"I was so scared of men"

Laura Wills, the youngest of Millie and T.C. Francis's eight children, was still living in Cleveland. Charlene told her I would call, and she had prepared herself. She'd talked it over with Charlene. She'd sought guidance from her pastor. She'd prayed to God.

By the fall of 2007, at her pastor's urging, she was ready to tell her story to me.

I didn't call. I wanted to meet Laura, but when I returned to Cleveland from Boston I was not ready. I felt upset and depressed by what Charlene and Philip had told me. I couldn't get the image of the boys hanging from hooks out of my head.

One week went by. Then two. I busied myself with transcribing the recordings and searching for records that weren't in the files I already had. I still didn't call Laura. Winter crept into Ohio. Masses of gray clouds parked themselves over Lake Erie and Cleveland, where they would stay through April.

Honking geese passed under them. After the cold came the snow.

Thanksgiving was approaching when I finally called Laura. She told me she'd wondered if I was ever going to call, and invited Lisa and me to come visit. The Monday after the holiday, we drove to her house on Cleveland Road in Glenville, a neighborhood of front-porch houses that had once been 90 percent Jewish and middle-class. Superman was born here, the creation of Glenville's Jerry Siegel and Joe Shuster. As the Second Great Migration brought a wave of black families from the Jim Crow South to industrial cities, the newcomers to Cleveland found that Jewish home owners were more willing to sell to them than others. In 1940, the neighborhood was 2 percent black; by 1950, as the Jewish population began to sell their houses and move to the suburbs, that number had risen to 40 percent. Today Glenville is 97 percent black.

Laura was ready for Christmas. Presents were wrapped and waiting under a tree, its blinking lights competing with the big-screen television. It was tuned to a televangelist, who preached with the backing of a full gospel choir. On one wall hung a painting of the Last Supper, surrounded by framed photographs of Laura and her husband, Gus, and their children. On a stand in the corner, a Bible was open to Psalms.

Laura sat on the couch holding her son, Keishaun. I sat next to them, balancing my recorder on the cushion in between. Keishaun snuggled his head against his mother's shoulder and coughed into her chest, the coughs deep and wet. "He has asthma bad," Laura said, patting his back. "I've got to give him a treatment in a little while."

"He's so cute!" Lisa said. "How old is he?"

"He'll be three in January," Laura said.

"He's big," Lisa said.

"Yeaaahh," Laura said, stroking his head. "He's still my baby."

I had seen the family resemblance in Charlene and David, but Laura seemed to come from a different family altogether. Her skin was much lighter, her hair straight. But it was the eyes that really separated her from them. Charlene and David had a hard, calculating gaze that unraveled me. Laura looked at me with eyes that were reserved but peaceful.

"So, you talked to Charlene," I said. "Did she tell you anything about what I'm doing?"

"That you're writing about my brother, about you being a survivor?" Laura said. "You were my brother's victim?"

Keishaun coughed. She shifted him on her lap. I nodded.

"I'm sorry to hear that," she said. "I didn't really know him. I distanced myself from my brother, growing up. He has always been disturbed, far as I know. In and out of prison, since he was twelve or so. He had attempts on my father's life. A couple of things in Boston I can remember hearing when I was a child, him being in jail. He's always been a problem child. I distanced myself from him. Far as it goes."

It almost sounded as though she had practiced it before we came over. I could tell she didn't want to talk about any of this.

"My father was an alcoholic; he was abusive to my mother," she said. "He would do things, tamper with me, and said if I told my mother he would kill me." She said this without emotion, reporting facts, exactly the way I told people about my rape.

"What do you mean, tamper with you?"

"I was so afraid of him where I automatically, when he came to the door, I would pee on myself. And that would make him angry, and he would drag me in the bathroom and my punishment, after he got through beating on me, I had to get on my knees and hold my face over in the toilet, the commode, until he decided I could come out of the bathroom. And every once in a while he would say, 'Laura, come here, Daddy want to check you and see if you peed on yourself.' And he would pull my pants down and stick his fingers, you know, and be playing with me down there."

When Laura was six years old and her brother Neamiah was eight, Millie Francis ran away from her husband, leaving them behind. The other children were grown and gone, or in juvenile custody.

"She told us she was going to the store, and she never came back," Laura said. "She left us with our father for a two-year period. And an incident happened. My father had got drunk, and he took me and threw me across the table and he broke my shoulder and my arm. And they got word to my mother—they found out where she was—and she came back to Boston and she took Neamiah and me away from him, and he told her if she ever came back that he would kill her. And the rest of us."

By then, Millie was going with a new man, Frank Rodriques, and had changed her name to Matia Rodriques so her husband couldn't track her down.

"They traveled a lot, her and this man," Laura said. "We went to Texas and Oklahoma, and came here to Cleveland, too. In Texas they had this little wooden church. Frank took me in the church, I remember him pulling my pants down and bending me over the pew, and he didn't molest me in my vagina." Laura paused and lowered her voice. "He did it rectally."

Laura was eight years old.

Her older sister Linda came to visit from Boston. "She was bathing me and I was all rough and raw down there. I told her what Frank did, and she told my mother, and my mother didn't believe me. She said, 'Stop lying, he's taking care of us.'"

They moved on, to Muscatine, Iowa. "Charlene came to visit, and she realized that it was still going on. So she called the sheriff, and the sheriff came out, and I had all kinds of people asking me questions, asking me to describe how big his penis was and asking me how it happened. And Frank just skipped town. We ain't seen the man since. I don't know if he's living or dead. After that it seems like my mother just started drinking and never stopped."

Millie took her two youngest children to Cleveland, where Charlene lived with her husband and infant daughter.

Charlene and Millie started going to the after-hours joint in the basement of Velma Chaney's house. There, Millie met Ida Taylor and her husband, and they introduced her to one of their friends.

"She met this man called Earlie B., and I don't know what this man had, but it was enough to make her not want to take care of her children anymore," Laura said. She didn't mention the glass eye, so I didn't, either.

"She just gave up on life," Laura said. "All she wanted to do was serve him and become an alcoholic and do what she wanted to do. She told me and Neamiah, 'I'm gonna let y'all stay with Velma for a while and then I'm gonna come back and get you.' Well, Velma went and got permanent custody so my mother couldn't get us back.'"

As foster kids, Laura and Neamiah brought in a monthly check for Velma. She also put them to work, cleaning the house and sometimes delivering the drugs Velma sold from her back door.

"We hated her," Laura said. "She used to call us little half-white bastards, 'cause of our light skin and straight hair. She beat me so bad with an extension cord you couldn't believe it—for getting the wrong thing at the store."

Neamiah ran away from Velma's house when he was four-teen and Laura was twelve. "I don't know if Charlene told you, but Neamiah is gay," Laura said. "And Velma caught him and some other boy having sex. So she made him dress up in one of my outfits, a dress, and parade up and down the street. After that, he told me he was going to a place called Safe Place for teenagers. I told him, 'Don't leave me alone.' He left 'cause he knew it was going to get worse, but he promised to come back and get me. I haven't seen him since."

I was beginning to see that Laura kept her distance not just from her family, but from her own history. As she talked, I could hear myself telling my story with the same distance, as though it had happened to someone else.

Laura met Gus Wills when she was fifteen. His family lived three doors down from Velma.

"I didn't know he liked me, I was so scared of men," she said. "I was timid. I was—I couldn't even look a person in the eye. I was scared of men because every one that ever came around, they molested me. So here comes this young boy down the street, he comes down and says, 'I want you to be my girlfriend.' Just like that! He didn't ask me, he just said, 'I want you to be my girlfriend.'" So that's what she did.

Laura started spending most of her time at the Willses' house. They were a good Christian family; Gus's grandmother was an ordained minister. They went to another church on Sunday, but they had a sanctuary in the back room of the house where they had Bible study and helped anybody who was in need of help.

Laura was in need of help. She loved going to Mrs. Wills's house.

When she was eighteen, she got pregnant. It was an accident, but it was not a terrible thing for Laura. "That's the only real love I ever knew: my daughter and my husband-to-be. His family kind of knew the abusive situation in the foster home, so his mother told me to bring the baby and move in with them. I moved in with them, and that's the best thing I could have done in my life."

Gus was away in the military, and after a couple of years he and Laura got married. He was posted to Germany, where they lived for six years. One of Laura's sons was born there. They saved money, and came home to a Cleveland that had been invaded by crack.

"I was going out partying with friends that I hadn't seen since I was overseas," Laura said. "And I heard about this crack stuff, and I'd go to these parties. Then one night I was so drunk, one of my girlfriends was like, 'Hit this and it'll sober you up.' And I said, 'No, that's that crack—they say you get hooked on that.' She said, 'You won't get hooked, it'll just help sober you up.' I tried it, and she knew that I had a little money, getting back from Germany, and she knew that getting me to use drugs, well, it would supply her. As it went on, the little bit I was trying, I didn't realize it was becoming an addiction."

It didn't take long before she ran out of money and started stealing. "I found myself doing things that I wouldn't have done if I had never made the choice to pick those drugs up. I would come in and take things out of my house. I stole from relatives, I stole from my children, their toys; anything I thought could be sold, I took. You have to be a real crazy-looking woman to be walking down the street carrying a TV. And the TV, you bought it for two hundred dollars and all you get for it is twenty."

When she ran out of things to steal and sell, she sold herself. "I did a lot of things that I'm not proud of," she said.

She had three children by this time, a daughter and two sons. She left them alone in the house while she went out to get high. She got into a lot of cars with a lot of men. Two of them raped her. When I asked if she had reported the rapes, she looked at me as if I was out of my mind. "I didn't want to go to jail," she said.

Laura continued as though she were testifying in court. In a monotone, she told me about losing everything. "That drug demon, it wanted what it wanted," she said.

It went on for fifteen years. Her fourth child was born with drugs in her system. "She's not right," Laura said. "She's what you call mentally retarded."

The hospital alerted Children and Family Services. The caseworkers determined Laura was neglecting the children. They came to the house and took the four children away from her and Gus. They were gone for twelve years.

Laura told me she thanks Jesus for their foster mother, who officially adopted all four children. She's a good woman and loved them, Laura said.

Her children gone, Laura went on using. Gus finally had to make her leave their house. She was homeless, sleeping in crack houses and cars. She went through a drug program, but only because it was a choice between the program or jail, and she started using again as soon as she was out. She was picked up for solicitation five times. One of those times a judge sent her to the workhouse for eight months, but she got out after two and a half for good behavior.

"I couldn't deal with being sober, because when I was sober I started thinking about my kids and crying," she said. "I didn't want to live like that. I could see myself dying in a crack house, and I didn't want to go that way."

Right before the new year of 2004, she called on God for help, even though she didn't really believe in any of that anymore. "But I came to the realization, I'm never going to see my kids, and the last time I got high, this guy raped me in the car, and afterwards he took all my clothes and my shoes and turned me out of the car. And something came over me, and it was nothing but God speaking to me and telling me to come out. I was tired. I had called on God, to give me a moment to make a decision, to take me away from this. I was homeless, it was in the winter, I was in the backseat of a car under a nasty blanket."

She went to her husband's apartment. "I asked him, could I come in and take a bath and get something to eat? And he said, 'Laura, I can't let you in. I got to show you tough love.' And I said, 'I'm tired. I really need to take a bath and use the phone and see if I can get some help.' And he said, 'If you're tired and you really want to get yourself together, first thing in the morning I'll take you and make sure you get help.' I took a bath, and he made sure I ate. And he watched me all through the night. I don't think he got no sleep."

The next day Gus took her to get treatment. "I did out-patient for six months, intensive treatment, going all day every day, and then I did three and a half months aftercare. Then I did meetings, which I still do meetings today."

She moved back in with Gus and started going to her church, Emmanuel Christian, but just off and on. She still didn't really believe. Then one day the drug demon came back and pulled her back out on the streets. The next night, she was walking along East 55th Street when a car pulled up and two women got out. It was the First Lady of their church—the pastor's wife—and Sister Janice. "I don't know how they found me, but First Lady said to me, 'God is working through me to bring you home.'"

She was almost three months pregnant and didn't know it. Gus was the one who figured it out. "He said, 'Laura, I can't lose another one of my babies. You got to figure this out.'"

She went to a Christian place for pregnant women and stayed away from home, away from the neighborhood and the drugs and the temptations, until Keishaun was born. Three hours later, a social worker came into her room and said they didn't find drugs in his system or her system, but, because of her history, they didn't think the baby could go home with her.

She was shattered. That's when she was finished with drugs at last.

"When I finally decided I wanted to get myself together, I asked the Lord if he helped me to stay clean and sober, I would raise my baby up in his house." Her pastor went to court with her to get Keishaun back.

Keishaun had fallen asleep on Laura's lap, slumped forward on her chest. Now, on cue, he woke up and started crying.

"There's a lot I've forgotten and blocked out," Laura said. "You start using drugs and drinking, you're burying that stuff."

CHAPTER TWENTY

A diamond in the rough

In the days before he found me, breathless and late for an appointment, David Francis had tried to make someone else his victim: his baby sister, Laura.

I put the pieces together as she told me about the last time she saw him, my adrenaline flooding as her memory took her closer and closer to July 9, 1984.

"Last time I seen him I had just had my first child," Laura said. "I was about nineteen. He had just got out of prison and he had been out about a month. The only time he came around and called, he called himself a pimp. He wanted me to meet him downtown, in a hotel. He had these guys down there, they was Mafia, he said, and he was going to turn me out and I was going to make money for him. And [he said] if I didn't do what he said, that he was going to kill me. And I could tell he was serious—he wasn't talking to me like a brother talks to a sister. And I told my mother, and the next time he called her she said to leave me alone or she would have him locked up again."

"Do you remember when that was?" I asked.

"It was right before my mother died. About 1984."

"Nineteen eighty-four. You're sure?"

"Yeah. She was still up here in Cleveland at the time, before my sisters took her back to Boston."

"Laura, that had to be in July, when he raped me. But he couldn't have been out of prison for that long. He was only out of prison for a week, and then they caught him the day after he raped me and he was back in jail. So he called you right before he found me. Then your mother died in August."

"They brought him in shackles to my mother's funeral," she said.

"I don't think so. He was here, in Cleveland, in the county jail. I think I would have heard if they let him go to Boston. Though actually, I've found out they didn't tell me everything, so he might have been there."

One of the things they didn't tell me was that they discovered a weapon on him in the county jail.

"It must have been Philip then," she said. "Yeah, it was Philip. They brought him with chains on his legs and arms, and three guards. That was the last time I saw my father, at my mother's funeral. It was awful. The city had to bury her because we didn't have the money. My father came, and sat right in the family row, right in front of my mother's casket. The exact words out of his mouth were, 'The bitch got what she deserved.' I told him, 'When you die, I'm coming to your grave long enough to spit on it.' And I never saw him again."

I was far more riveted by the way our orbits aligned back in 1984 than Laura was. She escaped her brother; I didn't. It made me wonder about David Francis's other victims. The cops had told me that rapists tend to be serial criminals, escalating the violence with each rape. They were speaking from anecdotal stories and their own observations, but the recent results of rape kit testing and research back them up.

In 2002, David Lisak of the University of Massachusetts and Paul M. Miller of Brown University School of Medicine reported: "Studies that use long follow-up periods tend to show alarming rates of sexual reoffending among rapists . . . (and) several studies have shown that among incarcerated rapists the actual number of sexual crimes committed far exceeds the number of adjudicated charges against these men."

Who else did David Francis rape or assault? I went back to see if I missed something in the criminal files from the prosecutor's office.

When he was seventeen, David Francis was arrested in Boston and charged with "unnatural acts." But because he was a juvenile, with more privacy protections under the law than adults, I could not get any more information on it from Massachusetts. Nor could I get information on another charge, made a week before the unnatural acts, for "assault in the 2nd degree" in West Hartford, Connecticut.

He was no longer a juvenile when he followed his mother to Cleveland in 1976 or 1977. He was twenty-one when his arrests in Cleveland started, nonviolent crimes that came one after the other. He would draw some jail time, get out, and do it again. Like his brother Philip, he changed his identity with nearly every arrest.

When he was arrested for receiving stolen property, he was Dalin Allen. When he was arrested for aggravated burglary, robbery, and carrying a concealed weapon, he was Daniel Allen. When he was arrested for breaking and entering, he was Tony Wayne. And he was Kevin Brown when he was arrested in Cleveland on January 22, 1978, for aggravated robbery, aggravated burglary, carrying a concealed weapon . . . and kidnapping.

I had missed the kidnapping charge the other times I looked at his records. As David Francis, he had limited his crimes to stealing cars and breaking into buildings. Except for the assault and unnatural acts charges when he was a juvenile in Boston, the kidnapping was his first crime against a person—at least, the only one I could find. What had he done to draw that charge?

I learned about the aliases in the file the prosecutor's office gave me, but in all of that, I could find nothing more about the kidnapping charge. There was no trial transcript, because he pleaded guilty. The police department couldn't find the thirty-year-old arrest report.

What exactly did Kevin Brown do? I decided to go back to see Russell Harrison, Ida Taylor's son, the one who said he couldn't remember David Francis on my first visit. Maybe his memory was bad, but records showed that the two had been arrested together in the fall of 1977 for a crime that carried more than a tinge of irony.

On the evening of October 11, 1977, the two broke into the Afro-American Historical and Cultural Society, founded and run by Icabod Flewellen.

Flewellen worked as a janitor at Case Western Reserve University, where he earned a BA in history at the age of seventy-six. Long before that, however, he began amassing a collection of items reflecting his life's passion, African-American history. He was single-minded but wildly indiscriminate, collecting valuable African art and significant historic artifacts and displaying them alongside unremarkable household memorabilia he gathered going door to door in Hough. His house looked like a hoarder's warehouse, the story goes, but he called it a museum and opened its doors in 1953. Though he moved it to several other locations over the years, he never quite achieved his dream of establishing an important cultural institution for the study of black history. Money to pay staff and fix leaky roofs was a constant problem, as was his habit of conducting one-sided feuds with his supporters.

He reported the break-in to the police, whose report does not show what, if anything, Russell Harrison and David Francis stole. I was disappointed to find that the report also did not record what Flewellen had to say about two young African-American men breaking into a museum dedicated to their own history.

I decided to see if Harrison's memory had improved since the first time I'd met him.

In the months in between, I had gone to see Ida in the hospital following her knee surgery, hoping she could tell me a little more about David Francis. She couldn't, but I stayed awhile to talk and she remembered my visit when I called to set up another meeting.

Lisa, who was not yet working with me the first time I went, came with me. Ida led us into the dining room. Russell was there, and so was Gregory, the brother I met on the first visit. They sat at the table with another son and a daughter, watching *The Twilight Zone* on a very large TV.

Ida sat at the head of the table, next to her daughter, who told us she was Gloria. The other son never spoke. They kept the TV on while we talked, adding a sci-fi sound track to the proceedings.

I asked them how long they had lived in this house.

"Oh, they call me the 'Queen of the Street,' I've lived here so long," Ida said. "We moved here in 1969. I've lived here longer than anyone else."

"This was a live street, back in the day," Gloria said.

"Yeah, them were the good old days," Russell said. "Partying, partying, partying."

"Everybody else is gone now," Ida said. "They died, they moved. More died than moved."

I asked if anyone else in the family had nicknames like Queen of the Street.

"We call her Big Momma, too," Russell said. "I'm the Godfather. If you want to write a book about me, you'd have to call it 'The Day the Earth Stood Still.'"

Everyone laughed. I didn't get it.

"I'm Mae West," Gloria said. "And Gregory there is Hubba Bubba."

Now I wondered if they were putting me on.

A young woman came in, gave Ida some cash, kissed her on the cheek, and sat down. "My granddaughter," Ida said with pride. The money must have been lottery winnings, because this set off a conversation that I recorded in my notebook only as "long discussion of lottery."

When they finished, I asked if they had remembered any more about David Francis since my first time there. I was saving what I knew about the 1977 arrest for later, if I needed it, but Russell surprised me.

Right off, he said, "Yeah, we ran together."

"Yeah, I saw that you were arrested together in 1977," I said.

He nodded and shrugged. "I wouldn't have a lot negative to say about him."

He flashed a smile at Lisa, who was standing in a corner with her camera. "Aren't you going to take my picture?" He managed to turn the question into a pickup line.

"Not yet," Lisa answered.

Russell looked back at me. "He used to be my protégé at the time."

Ida broke in to say that she hadn't remembered much about David when I first asked, but after I left she remembered more. "He was in and out of the house 'cause his mother lived here," Ida said. "His mom stayed here, he stayed here, Laura stayed here. . . ." She gazed off into the distance.

"So, was he your protégé in crime?" I asked Russell.

"Yeah," he said. "He was my protégé in crime—and the ladies." He winked at Lisa. His brothers laughed.

"What else did you do together?" I asked.

"I can give you information about myself, but I'll sell my story because my life is worth something," he said.

Then he looked at Lisa again and smiled. "But I can tell you that even when I was bad, I was good," he said, drawing out the last word so it came out "gooooooood." Now everyone laughed.

"See, I saw David as a diamond in the rough," he said. "I was basically schooling him. I went to prison for one robbery we did, and I didn't tell on him. I took the fall for it." He sat up straighter. "I was locked up for several years."

"Back in the day they was different than where they are now," Ida said, looking around at her sons. Gloria patted her mother on the arm and smiled. "You love your boys no matter what," she said.

"I was in Lima, I was in Mansfield," Russell said, ticking off Ohio prisons. "I been to a number of them. Last time I got out of the penitentiary, I said, 'I need a vet.'"

"A vet?"

"Yeah, you know, a veteran. An older woman who would take care of me," he said. "I had one once. She was a preacher."

He winked again at Lisa.

"Did you know David went to prison for rape?" I asked.

"No," Russell said, his tone neutral. "Last time I got out, I never saw him again."

"Are you surprised he was convicted of a rape?"

"Nope," he said. "In the process of doing this one robbery, there was a young girl, and next thing I know he's in the bedroom with her. In the bed. I said, 'C'mon now,' and he said 'No.' I had to get him out of there. So I knew it was inevitable."

"So you protected the girl?"

"Yeah. See, he might have had to rape, but I was an ex-player. Real good with the women. For me it was like apples in an orchard: I just reached up and plucked them off the tree."

He looked over at Lisa once more.

"It's just that I was charming, as you can well see."

"How long were you in prison?"

"Several years," he said. "See, I don't mind telling you I was in a penitentiary. A lot of people try to forget their past, but I think that's a mistake. 'Cause if you forget where you came from, you could go down that same path again."

His brothers and sister nodded in agreement. Russell repeated that I'd have to pay him to talk more. I closed my notebook. Lisa hadn't taken any photos yet, but she started to pack up her bag.

"You should come to my church," Russell said while I waited. He gave me the address. "I'm usually there, but if I'm not, just tell them Reverend Harrison sent you."

In the car, I said to Lisa, "Jesus, I thought he was going to ask you to go upstairs with him."

Lisa laughed. "Did you see the hands on that guy dressed as a woman?"

"What?"

"Gloria," she said. "That was a guy."

How could I have not seen that? I was focusing on Russell, but still. I was embarrassed I had missed something that was so obvious to Lisa. Gloria was the one who said she was called Mae West. All through the conversation, she sat close to Ida, patting her arm. I'd thought, *That's a good daughter*, and turned my attention to the wayward son.

"Her whole family accepts her," I said. "Wow. That's great—it's no big deal to them."

"I know," Lisa said. "Amazing."

When I looked Gloria up in the county's criminal database, I found something interesting. In both 1986 and 2004, when she was arrested for theft and, later, drug possession, the records identified her as male. But in 1986, the court sentenced her for the theft to the Ohio Reformatory for Women in Marysville.

I found it hard to believe the Ohio corrections system was that tolerant and forward-thinking in 1986, or even today, for that matter. It's possible Gloria had gotten sexual reassignment surgery, but I doubted it, given the expense. Later, Laura told me they might have sent her to Marysville before they realized she was a man, at least anatomically.

The next day I went to the Justice Center to see if I could find in the police department's records what Russell Harrison had been hiding. I left with copies of decades-old microfilmed documents from his police files. They were dark and blurred, as though they had been printed in disappearing ink. It took me hours to read it all, not just because of the dark copies but because my hands were shaking as I read.

The reverend had a lot to hide.

★

At lunchtime on Monday, August 29, 1977, the Reverend Thomas Gallagher answered the door to the rectory of St.

Philip Neri Church on St. Clair Avenue in Cleveland, where he was the priest. A young man stood in front of him. Gallagher thought he recognized him, maybe from his old church, St. Agatha on St. Clair and East 109th Street.

The young man asked the priest a couple of questions about church youth programs, then asked, "Can I use your bathroom?"

Gallagher hesitated. Did he really recognize this young man? Maybe he shouldn't let him in. But Gallagher ignored his instincts. He had worked in the inner city for years, it was his calling, and it did not feel right to suspect the young man. He let him in and pointed to the bathroom.

A minute later, the man came out of the bathroom holding a .38-caliber blue steel revolver. "I have a present for you," he said, pointing the gun at the priest's head. The man was David Francis.

Francis opened the rectory door and let in a slightly older man. Russell Harrison.

"Where is your housekeeper?" Francis asked.

The rectory had no housekeeper. Julie Casey was in the kitchen, making hot dogs for lunch. Julie was a volunteer, and only fifteen years old. It was her last day of summer vacation. Gallagher called to her, and when she came into the room and saw the two men and the gun, Gallagher was surprised by her reaction. She didn't seem to be afraid; she was angry.

"This is the third time I've been robbed this month," she said.

Francis turned to Gallagher. "You have three minutes to show me where all the money is."

Gallagher took them upstairs to his bedroom safe. Harrison stayed with him. Francis took the girl into another bedroom. After a few minutes, Harrison went to find them and discovered Francis holding the girl down on the bed. She was crying. Harrison ordered him back to the priest's room. "And bring the girl," he said.

As Gallagher opened the lock, Francis stepped behind him and cocked the gun at his head with a loud *click*. Gallagher would remember the sound of that click more than thirty years later, as clearly as he heard it that day. He took it as a warning: Don't try pulling a gun out of the safe.

Harrison heard the click, too. "Don't shoot the minister unless you have to," he said.

When the safe was open, the men made Gallagher and the girl lie facedown on the floor and bound their hands and feet. Then they took Gallagher's briefcase and filled it with the cash in the safe: $1,201 that had been collected at a bingo game and raffle the night before.

Harrison went through the priest's pockets, then the girl's, taking their cash. He took the watches off their wrists, a turquoise ring from Julie, and a gold pocket watch from the priest's dresser—a railroad watch inscribed "A.G."

They pulled the priest and the girl to their feet and ordered them into the closet. The priest remembered that with their ankles bound, they had to hop in. The men barricaded the closet with a dresser and some chairs and left. Later, two nuns said they saw them walk out of the rectory as though they belonged there. The priest waited a while after he heard them leave before he pushed out of the closet, cut his and Julie's hands free with scissors, and called the police.

★

Four and a half months after the robbery, the case was unsolved and Russell Harrison and David Francis were still free. Records don't show where Francis was, but Harrison was living on the east side of Cleveland with his new girlfriend, a woman he'd known for seven months.

The blurred microfilm copies of the police reports told the story of her two-year-old daughter, Jasmine.

On January 16, 1978, Jasmine wouldn't eat her dinner. Russell ordered her to eat, and when she wouldn't mind him, he slapped the toddler's forehead, making her fall back and hit her head. Jasmine's mother told the police that after this she went into the kitchen and said, "Jasmine, eat your food so your daddy won't get mad at you," which got her daughter to eat.

"He came in, and seen that she was eating her food for me," the girlfriend said, which made him even angrier. "And that's when he tied her up with a clothesline rope, and he picked her up and shook her and he said, 'Damn it, girl, you're going to mind me!' if he had to whip her butt every time she turned around."

This was at 7 in the evening, Jasmine's mother said.

The next morning, Jasmine lay unresponsive on the floor of her bedroom, which police later found empty of everything but a few pieces of her clothing, a potty-training chair, and a suede belt, which one of Jasmine's aunts told them Harrison used to tie the child to the potty. At the hospital, the emergency crew reported that he said, "If she lives, I promise I will never beat her again."

She did not live. In the five months that Russell Harrison had lived with his girlfriend, Jasmine, and her brother, "He whipped her about ten or eleven times," the girlfriend told police. "She would always make him mad, but he said that he liked the child."

In the dining room, the police found a gun and a splintered wooden paddle.

And in the closet in the room where Russell Harrison slept, they found items that had been reported stolen in August, six months earlier: a Timex watch with a gold band and a blue face, and a gold Illinois Central pocket watch inscribed "A.G."

★

Four months later, when Russell Harrison was in county jail for the murder of Jasmine, the police asked him about the gold pocket watch and the Timex they'd found in his closet.

Apparently, Harrison did not take the fall for David Francis, as he'd claimed. Five days later, police tracked Francis down. When they arrested him, he gave them an alias, Kevin Brown, and so it remains, to this day, in the county criminal database. He pleaded guilty to all the counts but kidnapping, went to prison, and was paroled. When that was is not clear in the records, but in 1982, he was back in prison for violating that parole. The next time he was paroled was in July of 1984.

When the prosecutor compiled the criminal record for David Francis's file, preparing to try him for my rape, the report on the robbery and kidnapping at the church rectory was not there. It was still in the record for "Kevin Brown," though that record does note that Brown sometimes used the alias Daniel Allen.

Harrison pleaded guilty to involuntary manslaughter for the death of Jasmine, and guilty to aggravated robbery for holding up Father Gallagher. He was sentenced to seven to twenty-five years on each count, to run consecutively. I could not find records of his release date, but I was stunned to see that he served less time for murdering a child than Francis did for raping me. Harrison was out by 1995, when he was arrested for drug abuse with violence specifications. On that charge, the court offered probation, with several requirements for drug rehabilitation. When he tested positive for cocaine in 1998, he was sent to prison. He was out again in 2000.

★

Father Thomas Gallagher, seventy-seven years old and retired, was worried when I told him that one of the men who tied him up back in 1977 was still alive and out of prison.

"When all this happened, I was thinking they might come after me because I was a witness," he said. Before we talked, he said, he needed to ask me: "If I say anything now, will he come after me?"

We were having coffee in the food court of Summit Mall, near Gallagher's retirement home in Akron. It was January of 2008. On the phone, Gallagher had told me to look for the "short Irish guy in the collar." I would have known him anyway, from the photo that ran with the story in *The Plain Dealer* the day after the robbery.

Father Gallagher told me he stayed on at St. Philip Neri after the robbery, leaving in 1990 only because he was reassigned to the Veterans Affairs hospitals in Cleveland. He retired in 2000 at the age of seventy, having spent more than twenty-five years ministering to the poor in inner-city parishes.

"Even before I was a priest, I felt strongly about interracial justice," he said. "I just happened to be ordained at the right time, when John the 23rd was pope. I was ordained in 1961, and Vatican II was right after that. It was a time when a lot of us in the Church were really fired up about integration and social justice. Changes were just starting to come."

When he was a seminarian he took urban studies courses at Case Western, and later he entered a four-year program created to teach clergy of all faiths how to organize for social changes in their communities.

"We did all kinds of radical things," he said. "Now, of course, we're thought of as too radical." In the decades of conservative popes who came after John the 23rd, the activist social justice and liberation theology movements in the Church had receded.

Father Gallagher took a sip of his coffee and looked around the mall. It was 10:30 in the morning, and except for us, the place was empty.

"I remember going to jail one time for ten days, so we could experience the conditions of our prisoners," he said. "It was my radicalization year."

In 1965, the bishop of the diocese forbade his priests to join in the civil rights actions in the South. Gallagher and another young priest defied his order and went anyway, boarding a plane on March 23, 1965, heading for Alabama to join the last leg of the third Selma-to-Montgomery march. Dr. Martin Luther King Jr. was on the same plane. He had taken leave of the march for one day to come to Cleveland as the guest of honor at a Nobel Peace Prize dinner organized by local clergy for the benefit of the Southern Christian Leadership Conference, and was heading back.

I asked if they'd talked. "Oh yes," Gallagher said. "He wanted to talk theology with us."

After that, Gallagher asked the diocese for assignments in the inner city, and got them, leading three churches in poor, mostly black neighborhoods. He joined the Council of Christians and Jews and the NAACP, and was on the board of the Urban League in Akron.

What David Francis and Russell Harrison did to him didn't stop him from his mission. I asked him if he was scared to be alone in the rectory after that.

At first he said no. "I was so happy they didn't kill us. At the time, with that big gun pointed at my head, I did think they would end up killing us. It seemed to me they were debating whether or not to do it."

The recording of our conversation lapses into several moments of silence.

"Did you pray during the break-in?" I asked.

"No," he said. "I wasn't praying. I was worried. I was thinking that I didn't have a will prepared."

"Did you ever get robbed again?"

"Well, after that we put bars on the lower windows but not on the upper ones. And one night someone put a ladder up and crawled in and took a TV and some clothes. I slept through it, and I was glad I did. But I was never mugged, and I took a lot of walks in the neighborhood. At another church, someone stole my car. On Ash Wednesday."

He paused. "You asked me if that break-in scared me," he said. "I didn't think I had any fears, but now that I'm thinking about it, I was always worried. There was always stress under the surface, and the stress lingers, and when you're driving around, you're always wondering, *Are they going to see me? Are they going to come find me? Are they going to do something to me so I won't talk?* I think that's when my diabetes started."

"What about forgiveness?" I asked. "Isn't that what a priest would tell someone, to forgive them?"

"Oh, I forgave them right away, when they didn't kill me," he said. "It didn't change my attitude about working and living in the inner city. I wanted to be there."

I had saved one question for last because I didn't want to make him uncomfortable. "Did you ever counsel any women in your churches who had been raped?" I asked.

It did make him uncomfortable. "I don't think so," he said. Then he looked down at his hands. "In seminary, we were taught to fear women," he went on. "We were taught to stay far away from them. They told us women are out to get you, they're out to get you in bed."

As I drove back to Cleveland, I felt light. Sitting there in that ordinary mall on an ordinary morning, drinking coffee with this short Irish man in a collar, I had that otherworldly feeling that sometimes comes in the presence of the extraordinary. I am not Catholic, or a believer in any other religion. But I felt as though I was meant to find Gallagher. We had glimpsed our own deaths in the face of the same man. I was meant to talk to him about fear and dying and forgiveness.

CHAPTER TWENTY-ONE

The Death House

When Judge Harry Hanna told David Francis, "I shall bury you in the bowels of our worst prison for as long as I can," he was referring to the Southern Ohio Correctional Facility. No one outside the offices of a state government building calls it that, though. Everyone calls it Lucasville, the name of the closest town.

The Appalachian South starts in southern Ohio, bracketed by West Virginia on the east and Kentucky to the south. It is Ohio's poorest and least-educated region, with poverty levels about double that of the rest of the state. In Lucasville and the surrounding area, the prison is one of the biggest employers.

This was where David Francis went in November of 1984, and this is where he stayed until the spring of 1993, when the longest and third-deadliest prison riot in the country's history erupted on Easter Sunday. For eleven days, about 450 inmates took over an entire cell block, holding a dozen guards hostage. When it was over, one guard and nine inmates were dead, and dozens injured.

It started when a group of Sunni Muslim inmates refused to undergo a tuberculosis test because it violated their religious beliefs. The warden had ordered that all prisoners would be tested, and decided to lock down the entire prison for the tests. Before the lockdown happened, though, the inmates responded to his order with violence.

But the TB tests were just the flash point that ignited the riot. The conditions had been smoldering for several years. The reports that came out in the wake of the riot noted a slew of troubling issues. The prison was overcrowded to the point that cells designed for one inmate housed two. The warden allowed phone calls only on Christmas Day. The inmate-to-guard ratio of 9 to 1 was dangerously tilted. Though smaller gangs existed, the Aryan Brotherhood and the Muslims ruled, and violent disputes between them flared often. The warden had eliminated the practice of inmates choosing their own cellmates, and randomly put together blacks and whites, lifers and short-timers, Aryan and Muslim. Though it was a maximum-security prison, it was run more like a medium- to low-security one, with guards moving hundreds of inmates to meals and work assignments at any time through the halls.

Former inmates told newspaper reporters about the conditions. "It's a hard joint," one of them said. "You have to live one day at a time at Lucasville. Everybody has a knife. And if you don't have one, you better get one." Then he demonstrated how to make a knife with a gallon-size plastic milk container and a piece of metal.

When I started my search, I wanted to know what paths David Francis and I had taken to bring us to our collision on

July 9, 1984, and where our lives went afterward. For him, the first nine years after the rape were spent living in a cramped cell, quite possibly with a member of the Aryan Brotherhood.

After the usual weeks of letters and phone calls asking for permission to visit the prisons where David Francis lived during the sixteen years after my rape, I went to Lucasville at the end of 2007. I hoped someone there might remember him.

I talked first with the warden, a man who had started his career as a guard and worked his way up the corrections ladder.

"It's important to understand the mission of Lucasville," he told me. The mission boiled down to this: Lucasville is the time-out chair for the problem children of the Ohio prison system. When an inmate at another prison is violent or disruptive, they ship him to Lucasville.

"We've got everybody's maladjusted here," the warden said. "That's all we have. And they come to Lucasville for serious things. They don't come here for singing poorly in the choir."

I was curious about how David Francis fit in with this rough crowd. "Is it true that other inmates treat the rapists worse than anyone else?" I asked.

"Well, that's kind of correctional lore, and in the past it was accurate," he said. "Sex offenders were not very well received by the other inmates. Now, though, so many more sex offenders are in prison, there's some normalcy to it."

I have been in prison visiting areas, rooms filled with inmates sitting with their wives or girlfriends, eating snack food purchased from the long rows of vending machines. They fiddle with their stacks of quarters and avoid looking at the other inmates and their visitors. No one has much to say.

This time I was going beyond the public area for a look inside what everyone considered the meanest prison in Ohio. Lisa was not with me—no photographers allowed. The spokesman guided me down the main corridor, where a line of inmates walked single file along the wall in silence.

"This is a lot calmer that I expected," I said.

My guide positioned himself between me and the inmates and shook his head. "Understand we're in a prison," he said. "It's deceptive. It's calm and orderly, but things do happen. It's no way to live."

No one could determine which cell, or even cell block, had once housed David Francis, so we went into a typical cell block. The cells, on two levels, surrounded an open control area. The guide told me that about half of the 1,460 inmates remained locked in these cells twenty-three hours a day, getting out only to shower and to exercise, alone.

We walked past the exercise area. In a small wire cage that brought to mind an animal display at the world's worst zoo, a man was doing pull-ups. As he went up and down, biceps ballooning, I saw he had a tattoo that curved around his neck, one word inked in elaborate Olde English lettering, the style of the Aryan Brotherhood: "NEFARIOUS."

The other, luckier inmates can leave their cells daily for jobs within the prison, and with good behavior are permitted group recreation time and meals in the dining hall. The average length of stay at Lucasville is about seven years.

I wore loose jeans and the baggiest sweatshirt I owned for this visit, an outfit that did nothing to stop the stares I drew everywhere we went. The attention unnerved me. I found myself calculating how many of these men might be in for rape, and moved closer to my guide.

We walked through the dining hall and the gym, and when we finished the tour, the guide surprised me with a question. "Do you want to see the Death House?" His voice was casual, like he was offering to show me the library. It surprised me. I knew Ohio executed its condemned prisoners at Lucasville and that reporters witnessed these executions. But I didn't know they let reporters all the way inside, past the designated viewing area.

Ohio, along with Oklahoma and Arizona, has become notorious for botching lethal injections, so much so that in 2015 the Supreme Court agreed to review the constitutionality of the procedures. The standard method involves three drugs, but a shortage of one of the drugs—created when the European supplier refused to sell it for use in executions—had led to improvisation.

In 2014, Ohio tried a controversial two-drug injection on one prisoner, a method never before used in the United States. The condemned man, sentenced to die for the rape and murder of a woman in 1989, died a slow and agonizing death, according to witnesses.

The most famous of Ohio's botched executions happened in 2009, when the executioners poked around for two and a half hours trying to find a usable vein in Romell Broom, who was sentenced to die for the rape and murder of a fourteen-year-old girl in Cleveland in 1984. Witnesses reported that Broom, who was grimacing and in pain, tried to help with the needle placement several times, pointing out possible veins and rubbing his arms. The governor finally called the execution off. In 2015, Broom was still on death row.

All of this happened in the years after 2008, the year of my tour. My guide led me across the yard to the door of a small, unmarked brick building and opened it. When I entered, I half expected to feel the presence of ghosts. I thought a place called the Death House had to be haunted by the spirits of unspeakable sorrow and dread.

But what struck me was how mundane it was. The institutional-beige walls and floors, the gurney, the medical equipment—these imitations of a hospital setting stripped the place of its power and meaning. They sterilized the act of killing a human being, transforming the enormity and mystery of death into a common medical procedure.

First we looked at side-by-side viewing areas, each the size of a walk-in closet, one for the inmates' witnesses and one for the victims'. They were separated by a thin wall, and in each, three worn vinyl office chairs faced the glass window that revealed the execution chamber. A hospital gurney outfitted with straps sat center stage, like a set piece in a play—an effect amplified by the curtains that could be drawn across the window when the drama ended.

We proceeded to the cell where the inmate waits for his execution, a small room with a bed, a sink, a toilet, and, hanging in an upper corner, a small TV. The TV made me want to cry. I pictured a condemned man spending the final hours of his life watching *Cops,* or *Judge Judy,* distracted to the very end.

"It is approximately seventeen steps from the cell to the execution chamber," the spokesman said. As we entered the chamber, bare but for the gurney, I saw a wall telephone installed for last-minute reprieves, and a microphone for the inmate to deliver his last words. The IV line and assorted medical devices were hidden in an adjacent room, which served as the equivalent of the blindfold over the eyes of men facing a firing squad.

I thought I detected the odor of gas in the chamber. I almost remarked on it, but I decided I'd imagined it, since they had never used gas for executions here. At one time Ohio gave the condemned a choice between death by lethal injection or death in the electric chair, but the chair had been removed several years before and donated to the Ohio Historical Society. They displayed it in 2011, in an exhibit that also included a wooden cage used on state mental patients in the late 1800s. It was called "Controversy Pieces You Don't Normally See."

I tried to picture the men who lay on this gurney and comprehended the inescapable and imminent certainty of their own death. Did they leave their bodies and hover above, watching and waiting? Did they think of their victims?

David Francis might have died here. My mother, my sisters, and my husband might have watched through the glass. My children might have never existed.

I could still smell the phantom gas as we left the building, still smell it as I said goodbye to the spokesman and walked to my car for the long drive back to Cleveland. The dark feeling I had expected in the Death House remained with me the entire drive north, as the late afternoon gave way to night and I passed the twin billboards of the Five Commandments.

★

David Francis remained at Lucasville for eight and a half years, until the Lucasville Uprising in 1993. Francis was not part of the revolt. On the fourth day of the rioting he was among the eighty-seven inmates who were evacuated to the now-closed prison in Lima. At the time, Lima warden Harry Russell said that the group included the most psychologically disturbed of Lucasville's inmates.

Francis, who was not a model prisoner, was moved from prison to prison when he got into trouble. A year after the move to Lima he was sent to the prison in Warren, and four years later, in May of 1998, he landed at his last prison, Lebanon, located between Cincinnati and Dayton.

In early 2008 I drove to Lebanon, traveling on an interstate with a legendary roadside attraction: Touchdown Jesus. He faced west toward the highway, positioned on an island between a megachurch's amphitheater and its baptismal pool, a magnificent sixty-two-foot Styrofoam-and-fiberglass sculpture. He appeared to be emerging from the earth, his arms raised to heaven in the gesture that referees use to signal a touchdown. Three years later, a bolt of lightning struck the statue, which went down in flames.

When I arrived at Lebanon, the warden had arranged for me to meet with three low-security inmates to talk about prison life. One of them, Holman, had been in Lucasville at the same time as Francis, but he didn't remember him.

"Now, rape is not considered that bad," he said, echoing what the Lucasville warden told me. "But back then, it was looked upon as the worst of the worst. On kids especially, but even on grown women. I would say his time was probably quite rough for that type of crime. He would have gotten no respect, and I'm sure he was preyed upon, just as he preyed upon you."

I knew Holman was trying to make me feel better, but it didn't work. I felt hollow. What difference did it make to me if other prisoners hurt David Francis? What was the point of any of it? American prisons and jails hold 2.3 million men and women. Counting various forms of community supervision outside of prison, 1 in 35 Americans was under some form of correctional supervision at the end of 2013, according to the Bureau of Justice Statistics.

They serve their time, most of them keeping their heads down or looking over their shoulders, just trying to make it through the threats and fights and dull routines of daily prison life. And then after a few years we let them out. But to what? What awaited David Francis when he was paroled in 1984? His mother was dying, his father was worthless, he had not finished high school, and he had a rap sheet that ran for pages and pages. What did anyone think he would do when he got out?

I couldn't stop thinking about the utter waste of that life, and all those lives, and when I visited Mansfield, another of David Francis's stops on his tour of Ohio's prisons, I said something to that effect to the warden.

"Don't feel sympathetic toward him," the warden said, looking at me with a stern expression. "Lots of people have hard lives, but they don't rape and murder other people. The guys in here? They deserve to be here."

Well, that was true, too. If they had not caught him after he raped me, the cops and the judge were sure he would have raped again, and possibly escalated to murder. He deserved to go back to prison.

Still, I kept thinking about what Philip said: "I didn't ask to be born. It's not my fault I was born. I still try to figure it out to this day: What did we do wrong to deserve such a tragic life?"

In it I heard an echo of *Paradise Lost*, when Adam asks God: "Did I request thee, Maker, from my clay to mould me man, did I solicit thee from darkness to promote me?"

Who was Top Cat but the maker of these tragic lives? Was he the one to blame for my rape, and whatever else David Francis did in his chaotic, violent life? Or did it go back to an earlier generation, to Top Cat's mother, the woman her grandchildren swear to this day was a witch? Or to his father, the ghost in the graveyard where Top Cat left his children crying in the dark?

How far back do you have to go to find the origin story of a monster?

Mary Shelley placed that quote from *Paradise Lost* at the very beginning of *Frankenstein*, one of the most famous of the monster-origin stories. But of course the monster of Shelley's gothic tale is not the unnamed creature. The true monster is his creator, Victor Frankenstein, the arrogant would-be God who assembles his creature from raw materials supplied by "the dissecting room and the slaughter-house," gives him life, and then—disgusted by his hideous creation—abandons him.

Like Top Cat Francis, Victor Frankenstein is a terrible father to his child. Any one of Top Cat's children could have said what the Creature says to Frankenstein when they meet at the end of the novel.

"I was benevolent and good; misery made me a fiend."

CHAPTER TWENTY-TWO
Digging up DAVE

By the winter of 2008, I had two places left to visit on David Francis's path.

The first was the Corrections Medical Center in Columbus, now called the Franklin Medical Center. The center is officially a prison, with a warden, corrections officers, many inmate counts through the day, and a locked-down maximum-security unit. But it also serves as an outpatient clinic, a hospital, and a nursing home.

David Francis died there at 11:10 a.m. on August 18, 2000. That's what his death certificate says, though when I went to visit the center in 2008, the assistant warden told me they had no record of him dying there. She checked with the corrections department. They had no record of him dying anywhere.

The death certificate reports his cause of death as unspecified Hodgkin's, the same cancer that had won him a mercy parole in July of 1984, the week before he raped me. It notes that they did not perform an autopsy. It lists his occupation as electrician, and his last known address as Lebanon Correctional. He was forty-four at the time of his death. He had been in prison for my rape for sixteen years.

If the certificate was right, he died in one of the two rooms at the end of a long hall that function as hospice rooms. As we made our way to them, past men in wheelchairs, the assistant warden said the rooms can't, legally, be called "hospice." I forgot to ask the reason.

We stopped at the last room. The door was open. From his bed, an old man raised his can of Coke to us in a toast and smiled. He had no front teeth.

"How are you doing?" the assistant warden asked.

"Oh, this is nice," he said, still smiling. "For a prison cell, you can't beat it."

Old men don't go to prison. Statistics show that the vast majority of inmates enter in their late teens and their twenties. It's likely this old man had been in prison most of his life. At the end, he found dying "nice."

The assistant warden told me that many of the healthy inmates who live and work at the center—a plum assignment— are trained to become ministers through Stephen Ministry, a Christian program that teaches laypeople to offer spiritual comfort during difficult life passages.

"They put on a vigil," she said. "Someone is always there, round the clock, so that the man will not die alone."

★

When David Francis died, he was awaiting his final parole hearing, the last of his many attempts to win freedom over the sixteen years. He first went up for a review consideration, the initial step toward an actual hearing, in July of 1991. Denied. Then again in 1995. Denied. A risk assessment form at that time noted that his alcohol usage problems ranked as the worst: "Frequent abuse, serious disruption, needs treatment." His drug problems ranked in the middle: "Occasional abuse, some disruption of functioning."

He could obtain both alcohol and drugs through the prisons' covert network. At the medical center, the assistant warden told me they get a lot of patients who have poisoned themselves with homemade hooch and contraband drugs.

In 1997, the parole board reconsidered whether to give David Francis a review hearing. His request was again denied. The next hearing was supposed to take place in July of 2000, a month before he died. No record exists to report whether the hearing was held, but in April of that year, they began the process for his review.

I found the parole documents in the file from the prosecutor. His prison case manager reported that in 1998 David Francis received nine days of disciplinary control for disobedience of a direct order and fifteen days for threats, and that in 1999 he spent ten days under disciplinary control for disobedience of a direct order and possession of contraband.

During his time in prison, he completed three programs: He got his high school GED. He participated in a weekend religious program called Kairos, described as "a short course in Christianity." And he went to a program described only as "Depression."

When I saw that notation on his parole report, I let out a bark of a laugh that made me think of Philip—a laugh that wasn't angry or bitter, and that definitely was not amused. It was a dead laugh.

★

No one claimed the body of David Francis. They called only Ida Taylor. She said, "You'll have to do with him what you do."

The State of Ohio sent him to a Columbus funeral home, where they put him into a plain pine casket. From there he went south, to the Pickaway Correctional Institution, just outside of the town of Orient. The grounds manager arranged in advance for a backhoe to dig his grave.

No family or friends came to his burial. As they lowered him into the ground, the prison chaplain said a few words. After two inmates filled in the grave, they sank a brick-size marker into the earth.

When I went to the Pickaway cemetery on a January morning in 2008, I was the first person who had ever asked to visit his grave. The day was clear but cold. The coils of razor wire surrounding the prison like a giant Slinky glinted in the weak winter sun. The frozen grass crunched under our feet as the prison investigator led Lisa and me up the hill.

At the top of the hill, under trees that spread their limbs over the dead, we came to the old part of the cemetery. The headstones, some with angels or lambs perching on them, date from the late 1800s, when this place was known as the

Orient Feeble Minded Institute and housed those with mental illness, mental retardation, epilepsy, and disorders that no one understood but were serious enough for families to commit their children. The name was eventually changed to the Orient State Institute, but the mission remained, even in 1950, to "care for the feeble-minded." It shut down in the early 1980s, one small part of the great wave of such closures across the country that were brought on both by revelations of terrible conditions at many institutions and government spending cuts.

In 1984—when the prison system was well on its way to becoming America's de facto largest mental health institution—the Orient State Institute reopened as the Pickaway Correctional Institution.

An invisible line separates Orient's pitiful dead from the graves of the unclaimed prisoners, who all lie in an open field on the hill beyond the old cemetery, 1,236 of them when I visited, their presence marked only by those brick-size stones. No angels or lambs watch over them. No one ever etched loving words on their stones. They don't even have names: In death, as in their life on the other side of the razor wire, they are identified by numbers. As the seasons change, grass grows over the small stones and covers even their numbers. The dead inmates disappear into the field.

David Francis, No. 130, was among those who had disappeared. The investigator said that the cemetery manager had marked the grave for me with a stake tied in yellow and red ribbons. I didn't see the stake, so I hunched over and walked up and down what seemed to be rows, pushing away leaves and grass. I eventually found 133, but it did not lead to 130 in any direction. The investigator, who didn't see the stake, either, went to call the manager while I paced off what seemed the right distance, bent down, and started pulling at the matted grass where No. 130 should have been.

I uncovered a tiny corner of stone, grabbed a stick, and kept digging. The stick broke. I dropped to my knees and dug in the dirt with my hands again, uncovering more stone. The earth was as cold as it was hard. My frozen fingers clawed at it, my nails breaking as I dug.

It took a while, kneeling there in that cold graveyard, for me to realize what I was doing.

I was trying to dig up DAVE from the place he was buried.

The investigator returned with the cemetery manager, who pointed at the stake at the far end of the field, about fifty yards from where I was digging. I walked over; the two men hung back and let me go alone. So did Lisa.

They had already uncovered it for me. I looked down at the stone: No. 130. After having spent eighteen months looking for this man, only now did it occur to me that I'd never thought about what I would say, or even what I might feel, when I found him. I felt that the occasion called for something—a ritual, a pronouncement, some acknowledgment that my rapist and I were sharing the same patch of Earth again.

Minutes passed. The men were silent, waiting. A wind had come up, cold and damp, as though signaling me to hurry along. I decided I should say something, so I looked at "130" and said, "Well, Dave, Charlene and I are the only ones who really thought about you after you died."

Talking to him that way felt contrived. From twenty-three years in the past, a memory appeared—of my newborn son, sitting on my lap, intent on my face as I conduct an awkward conversation with him. I cried then, but I did not cry now at the grave of David Francis.

I was cold. I had nothing to say. I thought of Laura, vowing to spit on her father's grave, but I did not feel her anger. I just wanted to leave the cemetery and its ghosts, and go instead toward warmth and life.

★

As a reporter, I have gone to cemeteries with grieving families. I've listened to them talk to their loved ones at the grave, watched them plant flowers and pull weeds and carefully place mementos. Once I went with a mother whose son had died of a heroin overdose at the age of twenty-one. She parked near her son's grave, opened the door, and played Phish from her car's CD system at top volume, filling the silent cemetery with the music he loved.

I understand the comfort and meaning a grave can offer mourners, the physical place it gives them to make a spiritual connection. I envy those who believe that life continues after death, that the people we loved are waiting for us across a wide river. For them, death is a beginning, not a terrible mystery that we fear and deny and will never solve.

I don't believe the dead can hear us speak, or watch over us, or wait for us. I don't believe that anything meaningful remains in their graves. I don't believe we have souls that will live on somewhere else after death.

All I know is that the dead live on within the people who remember them. They come back to life when we think about them.

I had kept David Francis alive, all this time.

CHAPTER TWENTY-THREE

"Why do you want to know anything more?"

Not long after finding his grave, I decided I had one more place to visit. I had to go back to Eldred Theater, where David's and my paths had collided.

I had not been there since July 9, 1984. A sense of foreboding emerged from the past and cast its shadow over me as I thought about going through that door again.

"I dread going back," I told Lisa.

I dread Eldred. How odd I had never noticed the pun.

I returned to the theater in late January, on one of those Cleveland days that come in a dozen shades of gray, turning the campus into a living daguerreotype. Students walked through the quad carrying their massive backpacks like Sherpas, heads down against the sleet.

The manager met me at the top of the stairs and let me go into the theater alone. It was dark, lit only by the ghost light in the middle of the stage. The single bulb glowed like an eerie beacon, leaving the edges and corners in deep gloom. I felt a charge in the air.

Some say ghost lights originated in Shakespeare's time, when theater companies left candles on the stage to ward off the ghosts of performances past. I had no doubt that the ghosts of my past lived here, in this haunted place.

I walked down the aisle. Lisa waited at the back, near the entrance, her camera still in her bag. I needed to be alone on that stage.

When I climbed the three steps up, the ghost light cast a huge, hulking shadow of me on the back wall. I walked toward the back corner where David Francis had dragged me. My shadow followed me, a giant bodyguard hovering over each step.

Painted scenery flats leaned against the wall in stacks, crowding the corner. I tried to see the stage the way the hundreds of students and actors and stagehands had seen it over the years—as a place to perform, nothing more.

But to me this was sinister and sacred ground. Here was the place where I had been certain my life would end, the place where I lost part of myself.

I felt disoriented, but my body was alert, flooded with an anxiety that made my knees lock. I sat on the edge of the stage to calm myself.

I thought about my children.

I used to wonder if, in trying to hide my depression and fear from them, I had instead passed it all on, like a genetic disease. Not long ago I read about a study that suggested I probably did pass it on to them—not *like* a genetic disease, but *as* a genetic disease. This study, conducted by a team of psychobiologists and published in the journal *Biological Psychiatry*, showed that rats subjected to stressors before they got pregnant passed that stress on to their offspring—not through anxious parenting styles but biologically, at the molecular level.

I suddenly wanted to ask my children, "Was I a good mother to you?"

This is a question that has only one answer. I know they would tell me that yes, I was a good mother. I am the only one who dares to say "No." That answer comes from the piece of me that lives inside, the piece that is afraid and wants me to hide from the many dangers of life.

That piece of me is afraid of so much, but what she most fears is that I am not good enough. That piece whispers that I am a fraud, that I will be revealed one day, that I am damaged and I damaged my children. That piece always looked at other families and decided they were perfect.

The tears that didn't come at the grave of David Francis ran down my face.

I thought about my husband, who had gone through the misery following the rape with me, and had gone through the silence that lingered. I thought the rape was mine alone, but I was wrong.

In the end, my husband and I divorced, for this, and the hit man, and many other reasons, most of them my fault. I did not treat him well when he wanted to protect me in the years that followed the rape. We separated while I was investigating David Francis, but even then, he helped me by showing me how to get the prosecutor's files and where to go for the trial transcript.

Sitting there in the dusky theater, I realized why I had not felt anything when I stood at David Francis's grave. That cemetery was where the prison had buried him. But here, in this theater, was where I had buried him. I had gone out to find David Francis. I thought if I unearthed his story, I could discover the reason that our paths crossed. And if I knew and could understand that, I could protect my children.

I had found David Francis. I learned that he had a horrifying childhood, that he learned violence from his father, and that he took that violence and damage with him when he went out into the world at the age of twelve.

I did not deserve what happened to me, as Charlene said.

And David Francis did not deserve what happened to him.

When I started my search, my husband said, "He's a monster. Why do you want to know anything more?"

I think the answer is that I wanted to know the monster in myself, the monster born in 1984. This monster is clever. Elusive. It doesn't show itself by taking a child into a church to rape her, or beating a son. This monster lurks so far in the background, no one knows it's there. It infused me with fear, a fear that made me hide from the world and harbor malign suspicions of other people.

Not long ago, a small benign cyst I had had on my neck for years started to get bigger. It doubled in size, tripled, and then turned red and tender. I made an appointment at my clinic, and the first doctor available turned out to be from Germany.

"Why are you in Cleveland?" I asked, the question all Clevelanders ask people who have moved here.

As he bent to my neck and prodded at the lump, he told me doctors can do more good in the United States than in Germany.

"Everyone should have access to good health care," he said. He told me he volunteers at the Free Clinic, and he can't believe what he sees there. "Hardly anyone knows that we have a third world right here, a few miles away, in the wealthiest country in the world. I mean, poverty that people wouldn't believe, right under our noses."

He rolled back on his little doctor's stool to the computer. "I'm going to refer you to Surgery," he said. "That cyst is infected. It should come out."

This sounds like something a writer would invent, a tidy symbol, but it is true.

The cyst had grown on the side of my neck right where David Francis had cut me. Two weeks later, a surgeon cut out the cyst and told me it was too infected to stitch up. Another infection could bloom, making it worse. Even though the wound was quite deep, he had to leave it open to heal, from the bottom up.

"It might leave a scar," the surgeon said.

It did. The scar is faint. Only I can see it.

★

I went out looking for David Francis, but during my search I found what I was really looking for all along.

I found Charlene, who stopped doing drugs and drinking, got her family back, and in time forgave and buried the father who hurt her. Charlene, who reacted to her rapes with the same shame and self-blame I did.

I found Laura, who took me to the church that had saved her, and pushed me to the altar when the time came for saving me. Laura calls me "sister" and "sweetie" every time we talk. She tells me she loves me.

I found Father Tom Gallagher, who marched from Selma to Montgomery with the Reverend Dr. Martin Luther King Jr., and would not let being held at gunpoint, tied up, and locked in a closet stop him from doing what he was put on this Earth to do.

I needed to hear their stories. They needed to tell them.

"We did our part; we kept it inside so long," Laura said to me. "It's something that needed to be told."

I've gone to Laura's church many times, even though I don't have the religious faith that she has. I often wish I did. I find my faith in the power of stories to bring us together and heal. As a reporter, I have asked so many other people to open themselves up and let me tell their stories, all the while withholding my own. I owed this to them. I owed it to other women who have been raped. I owed it to my children.

As I worked on the story that went into the newspaper, I kept saying, "I'm having a hard time with this. I can't write it." My therapist said, "Maybe you're saying, 'I can't right it.'"

Maybe.

And maybe that is the point, in the end. James Baldwin wrote, "Whatever one's journey is, one's got to accept the fact that disaster is one of the conditions under which you will make it."

We all have burdens we carry through life, grief and disappointments that we can't change. But we can make them lighter if we don't hide them, if we don't try to bear them silently and alone.

I cannot protect my children. I know this. It is the terrible truth of being a parent: The day comes when we have to send our very hearts out into the world, unprotected.

That day came while I was working on my story. They are out in the world now, in cities so far away I have to board a plane to see them. I try not to do it too often. They don't want my protection, any more than I wanted my husband's protection after I was raped.

They are smart and funny. I look at them with amazement and pride, most of all because they are kind to everyone. My son works as a lawyer for the homeless and for poor tenants facing evictions. My daughter studied psychology and plans to train to be a therapist.

They have some of me in them, and though I can disappear for hours into deep pools of guilt over some of what I passed on, they don't seem to mind.

They had veto power over the story that ran in *The Plain Dealer* in May of 2008, and over this book. They did not ask for any changes. My daughter cries when we talk about the rape. My son doesn't like to talk about it.

I know now that while I was focused so intensely on protecting them, my children were also protecting me, all those years. They tethered me to all that is hopeful. They made me brave. They held me to this life until I was ready to come back to myself.

Sitting there in Eldred Theater, I looked back up into the fly space. What happened to me in 1984, when I floated up there, has a name: disassociation. It's a well-known psychological term, though I didn't know it back then. Disassociation is how our psyches protect us from experiencing trauma we can't handle. It removes us from the event and gives the pain to someone else. That someone else is us, floating somewhere above.

She was up there. She was always up there, watching me, removing me from my life. She helped me push away the pain I was afraid to experience but needed to experience. The Buddhists' First Noble Truth says: Life is suffering. They teach that we live fully only when we stop pushing the pain away and accept that suffering is part of life.

I looked up again. I'm OK, I told her. You can come back now.

Acknowledgments

This book started as a story for the *Cleveland Plain Dealer*. My gratitude goes to my editor, Debbie Van Tassel, who wisely stopped me from trying to write about myself in the third person and kept me going; Susan Goldberg, who gave me time and support; Debra Adams Simmons, who made the book possible; Karen Long, my wise reader; and Lisa De Jong, an artist and a comrade. Thanks also to Clara Roberts, Stuart Warner, Wendy McManamon, Lynn Ishay, Madeline Drexler, and Rosie Kovacs.

I still can't believe my good fortune to have Elisabeth Schmitz as my editor and Grove Atlantic as my publisher. Through many drafts, Elisabeth's sensitive editing and kind, calm manner helped me transform a newspaper story into a book, and Katie Raissian's editing and enthusiasm came at just the right time. Thanks also to Morgan Entrekin, Deb Seager, Justina Batchelor, and to my agent, Jane Dystel, who led me to them.

Cuyahoga Arts and Culture gave me a generous Creative Workforce Fellowship grant just when I needed it. Thanks to everyone at CAC and the Community Partnership for Arts and Culture.

The Cleveland Rape Crisis Center was there for me from the beginning, and still is. Thanks to Sondra Miller, Megan O'Bryan, Kirsti Mouncey, Sarah Trimble, and all the staff and volunteers at this wonderful and necessary healing center.

My deepest thanks and love to Laura Wills, Charlene Blakney, Pastor Anthony Singleton, and First Lady Pam Singleton, and everyone who welcomed me at Emmanuel Christian Center, and to the Rev. Thomas Gallagher.

Thanks also to: Larry Donovan, Richard Thoma, the University Circle Police Department, Judge Harry Hanna, the doctors and nurses at University Hospitals Case Medical Center, Sue Johnson, Debbie Axelrod, Meryl Johnson, Diana Tittle, Marcie Goodman, and K.J. Montgomery.

I've saved my most important thanks for last.

To Dan and Zoe, who make me proud and fill me with love. To Chris, who stood by my side.

To Nancy Connors and Claire Connors, both generous with their advice, their unshakeable support, and their memories. They are first-rate writers and readers, and even better sisters. And in memory of our one-of-a-kind mother, Susie Sterrett Connors Mackenstadt.

This book truly would not exist without Jim Robenalt, a historian and writer of extraordinary books, who showed me how to do this by his example, encouragement, and love.

Finally, to all the survivors. And to the lovely, lost girls.